CONT[ENTS]

PART IV: ABOUT TIME

PART V: THE UNIVERSE AS ONE

PART VI: THE THEORY OF THE SOUL

UNIVERSAL AWARENESS:
A THEORY OF THE SOUL

SECOND EDITION

MICHAEL HEAP

UNIVERSAL AWARENESS: A THEORY OF THE SOUL
SECOND EDITION

Universal Awareness: A Theory of the Soul was first published in 2011 (CreateSpace, self-publishing). The present volume is the product of much revision and addition to the original material, and some omissions.

----0----

Michael Heap is a clinical and forensic psychologist with over fifty years' experience working both with people with mental health and neurological problems and with criminal offenders. He is now retired. An internationally recognised authority on hypnosis, he is also a prolific writer and speaker on skepticism and is chairman and secretary of the Association for Skeptical Enquiry, which he co-founded in 1997. He and his wife Valerie live in Sheffield, England, where he works in a voluntary capacity as a Humanist pastoral carer and school speaker. His website is http://www.mheap.com/.

Previous books written or edited by Michael Heap

Hypnosis: Current Clinical, Experimental and Forensic Practices

Hypnosis in Therapy (with H.B. Gibson)

Hypnotherapy: A Handbook (with W. Dryden)

Hypnotherapy: A Handbook, 2nd Edition

Hypnosis in Europe (with P. Hawkins)

Hartland's Medical and Dental Hypnosis, 4th Edition. (with K.K. Aravind)

The Highly Hypnotisable Person (with R.J. Brown and D.A. Oakley)

Hypnosis: Theory, Research and Application (with I. Kirsch)

PART VII: FURTHER EXPLORATIONS OF UNIVERSAL AWARENESS

APPENDICES

PROLOGUE

When I began working on the first edition of this book, it was with one simple question in mind: What happens to us when we die? Is it the end—oblivion—or does our soul, in the sense of our 'awareness of being', continue to exist in some form? This is an eternal question and most religions provide us with their own answers, usually describing some form of afterlife. Thousands of books have addressed this question, but often their authors have started out with the answer already in mind; their aim is then to present information and interpretations of that information that will convince the reader that theirs is the correct answer.

I believe I am being honest when I say that I did not set out to demonstrate the truth of any answers that I had already decided upon. I arrived at my answers by endeavouring at all times to follow a rational, logical, and evidence-based path and to avoid making any claims that are contradicted by the knowledge and understanding of our world that we owe to science. Thus, you may say that I embarked on 'a search for answers' and indeed I described the book as 'a journey of exploration' on which I invited the reader to accompany me as their guide.

In the years since publication of the book in 2011, I have continued to think about the questions I raised and the answers I provided; to study the feedback, both positive and critical, that I have received from readers; to further my knowledge of relevant matters through the writings of scientists and philosophers, particularly those that have appeared since my book's publication; and to discuss these matters with colleagues and acquaintances who share my interest, though not necessarily my conclusions.

Much of the material in the first edition is preserved here, though with updates, clarifications, and further elaboration where I have deemed this desirable. The most significant difference is that I have found it necessary to give much more attention to the distinction between 'the real world' and 'the world create by the brain (or mind)'. I have made clear where I stand on this important matter, and I find it necessary to make reference to it throughout the book. I have also gone into greater depth in support of the idea of representing the universe as one organic whole and considering any activity in it as an activity of the universe itself.

I confess that from the start I have been troubled by the term 'universal awareness', which many readers, on first encounter, may interpret as a vague, quasi-religious or New Age construction. In the years when I was writing the first edition (2000-2010), my Google searches yielded few references to this term, but since then the number of sources and meanings has grown (I claim no responsibility for this). I am not inclined to use a different expression now, but as before I stress that I have been at pains to ensure that the arguments I present are logical and rational; are not reliant on any paranormal or supernatural ideas or entities, mysterious forces or energies; and do not contradict our existing scientifically-based knowledge of the world. Despite this, nowhere do I claim to have constructed 'a scientific theory'; indeed I explicitly deny this.

The expression 'universal consciousness' is now frequently used in relation to the doctrine of panpsychism, the notion that 'having a mind' is a property applicable to all objects or matter in the universe. This is taken seriously by some philosophers, and indeed scientists, while others dismiss it as nonsense. I have not promoted my theory as panpsychic, but in this book I deliberate on the possibility of representing 'awareness' along a continuum or spectrum and thus displayed in varying measure by matter throughout the whole universe. I offer as a basis for this spectrum a broad interpretation of the biological property 'environmental sensitivity'.

In this revised edition, I have less to say on the subject of free will than in the 2011 book; in fact I do not cover this at all. Previously, I adopted the hypothesis that what we experience as being 'free to make a conscious choice' may apply to those instances where a single action is required and we are uncertain how to respond (the example I chose was pressing a button to detonate a bomb). I suggested that this uncertainty of outcome exists at the most basic physical level within the physiology of our brain, but when an outcome does occur, one way or the other, we interpret it as our exercising 'free will'. I also ventured a 'many worlds' interpretation where, figuratively speaking, in another universe the alternative outcome has prevailed. I am aware that some scientists speak in similar terms, so I claim no originality for these speculations.

I have not considered it essential to the main themes of the present edition to replicate this material; the interested reader may consult the original book. It is worth adding, however, that in everyday life, the choices we make (or appear to make) are determined by a myriad of interconnecting factors, including our interactions with other sentient beings, and can't be reduced to simple either/or decisions as exemplified by the press of a button (see Tallis [2019] for further discussion). Moreover, in the world of terrestrial humans, the range of things each of us can choose to do has escalated rapidly over time. We are inclined to forget this when, for example, we talk about people being responsible for the choices they make. Some have more choices than others.

The final part of this book (Part VII) contains new material unrelated to the initial questions that I set out to explore but which I consider deserves to be included if the idea of universal awareness is to be taken seriously. Specifically, I expand on the thesis that conscious awareness is a natural property of the universe and has an inherent tendency to be self-preserving and to expand over time, and this allows speculation on its future development.

At the end of the book I provide a much more condensed list of reading material than previously, focusing mainly on authors mentioned in the text.

So far as the conclusions that I reached in the 2011 edition, I have not found it necessary to alter these in any significant way.

Guidelines for the reader

In the 2011 edition, by way of preparation I set out some guidelines for the reader before embarking on 'our journey'. They are still apposite and I repeat them now with minor modifications.

There are six stages of our journey. At each stage we shall explore ways of thinking about our world that, although not grounded in any particular scientific theory, are at least consistent with current scientific knowledge and rational thinking. We shall also examine various philosophical paradoxes and conundrums that have important bearings on our questions. You will not be asked to accept any unlikely assumptions or to place any blind faith in what I am saying. Nevertheless, as our journey progresses, we shall have to consider ways of looking at our world that are radically different from how we usually do so in everyday life. You may be familiar with these ways of thinking, or they may be new to you. Whatever the case, I hope that, like me, you find them profound, exciting, and challenging. Even if, by the end of the book, you have reached conclusions that are different from mine, I am confident that you will have found this journey worthwhile.

I have avoided burdening you with references to the existing literature as we proceed. Where I do give a reference—name of author(s) and date—the source will be found in the reference list at the end of the book.

Questions

If you have never asked yourself the following questions, why not do so now?

Why was I born the person I am? Why wasn't I born somebody else? For example, the person next door; a person in another country; a person more fortunate than me; a famous person; a person who lived in the past; a person who has yet to be born; perhaps even another species of animal; or a being on another planet.

Do these questions have an answer? Do they have any real meaning? Or is it that they are based on a faulty understanding of our world, and when we think of the world in the correct way, the questions just go away? Whatever the case, let's carry on with our questions.

What happens to me when I die? I don't mean, of course, what happens to my body; I'm referring to what we often call 'the soul'. What happens to my soul when I die? Does my soul live on? And what happens to the people I know when *they* die? Do *their* souls live on somewhere? Shall my soul ever meet their souls again?

When we ask these questions, we usually think of 'the soul' as the individual person we are, but somehow without a physical body. Thus, we ask ourselves whether it's possible for our soul to outlive our body—say, to go to Heaven or Hell or to 'the other side' (and thus, perhaps, communicate in spirit form with those who are still living, as claimed by spiritualists and mediums).

There is however another way in which we can think of the soul. Consider the following question which people often ask themselves. 'Can my soul live on in the form of another person, so that after I die I am born again—reincarnated—as another individual (without necessarily knowing I was previously someone else)? Indeed, have I lived as someone else *before* being the person I am now?'

'Transmigration of the soul' assumes that the soul is immortal; it is a belief common to certain religions (and was also adhered to by some philosophers in ancient Greece, such as Pythagoras). Notice that when we are considering this, we imply a different meaning of 'the soul' than in our previous question. 'Soul' here refers to our 'awareness of being' or the sense of who we are, not the person whom we are aware of being.

Suppose the answer to the above question is there is no reincarnation of the soul. This now raises another question. If I never experienced self-awareness before I was born, and will never again experience it after I have died, does this mean I have only one chance of living as a conscious, self-aware being, namely the individual I am now?

If that is so, then another question arises: what is it that decided that I would be the individual I am and not some other person—John Smith, Nita Patel, Olga Schmidt, someone living 5,000 years ago or 5,000 years from now?

And there are more questions we can ask. If I only have this one chance of experiencing being a person (or any sentient being) would I have lost that chance if the person I am had never been born? After all, a lot could have happened to prevent my coming into the world. For example, my parents might never have met; they might I have decided to have no more children before I had the chance of being conceived; they might not have engaged in the physical act that created the person I am (or they might have used contraception); or I might have been aborted in my mother's womb. And what if a different sperm had fertilised the egg?

If any of these things had happened, would I have lost the opportunity of experiencing being a person? Or would I still have been born, but as someone else (a different 'me'). And if so, what would decide which person I would be born as instead?

The meaning of 'soul'

In this book it is the second of the two meanings of 'soul', namely our 'awareness of being', with which we shall be concerned, and not 'soul' in the sense of the *person* we are aware of being. Either way, the answer to our questions may simply be that we only live once, as the person we are, and then we die. And death is oblivion, as when we are rendered unconscious, but without return to any kind of awareness.

I propose we make the above our default position and resolve not to entertain seriously any other possibility unless and until we have accumulated enough evidence or justification for doing so.

Meditation

Now I have introduced you to all the questions which we shall be contemplating, I invite you to pause and spend some time mulling them over before proceeding on our journey. Do they make sense to you? Where do you stand at the moment? Do any further questions come to mind?

PART I

PREPARING THE WAY

CHAPTER 1

THROUGH A GLASS DARKLY[1]

Before embarking on a long and sometimes difficult journey it is important to devote enough time, thought and energy to making all necessary preparations. Now, for most journeys that we shall ever make we already know where we are starting from, and in which direction we should head off. In addition, we should be clear about what materials and methods we shall rely on to sustain and guide us and what rules and principles we need to adhere to. So from the start it is crucial that we recognise an important distinction that will come up time and again along our way. The distinction in question is that between the world as we consciously experience it and how the world is in reality.

Does reality exist?
It may seem strange for me to impress upon you that the first decision we must make before embarking on our journey is whether what we observe 'outside of us' actually exists! Yet I

---

[1] St Paul: 'For now, we see through a glass darkly.' 1 Corinthians, 13:12, King James Version.

expect that from time to time, like me and probably most people, you have been in a situation where you have asked yourself the question, 'Is this really happening or am I dreaming?' Let's say for example that you are witnessing an event so extraordinary that you say, 'I can't believe my eyes'; perhaps the shock of the experience lends it that dreamlike quality, and if it is something very unpleasant you might even hope that 'it's all a dream' and you will soon wake up. By thinking in this way, you are making a distinction between 'the world out there', or 'reality', and the world 'in your head', the world that your brain constructs. In the above example of observing the extraordinary event, if this were happening in reality then unless it requires your participation, it would still be happening even if you were not present to witness it.

You may have occasionally taken this line of thinking further and asked yourself, 'Is *everything* I experience just a dream?' In other words, does the world out there really exist independently of you or is there only one world, 'the world in your head'. Note that this 'world in your head' includes all the people around you, even loved ones; although they appear to be sentient beings with minds like yours, they are also only elements of a permanent dream you are having.

The above philosophy is akin to *solipsism*, the belief that the only thing a person can be sure of is that he or she exists; true knowledge of anything else is impossible. You might like to think about what the consequences would be in your life if you committed yourself to this way of thinking. Although to most people it seems highly unlikely to be true, it is not possible to disprove. You may say to me, 'I can prove you're not just imagining everything by stabbing you with a pin; the pain you would surely feel would demonstrate that the world is real and you are not dreaming it.' But pain itself is a private, subjective experience and could still be part of my dream.

A second possibility we might entertain is not to deny that minds other than our own exist but to assert that there is still no true, objective reality: the only 'real world' is the one that each of us constructs in our heads and no one's 'real world' is truer than anyone else's.

There are several arguments for believing that external reality exists; although they are not proofs, people find them very compelling. The first is that we have sensory organs— eyes, ears, a nose, a tongue, and tactile receptors—that appear clearly designed to respond to information external to us. This information is then conveyed via nerve fibres to our brain. If the world we experience were merely a dream generated by our brain, as dreams are, what would be the point of having these receptors?

Another reason for believing that reality exists is 'the uniformity of Nature'. What we experience as 'the world out there' is consistent and predictable; whatever happens does so in accordance with our knowledge of the world based on our previous experiences and those described by others. More formally, this knowledge includes logical rules and what we term 'laws of Nature' or 'scientific laws'. When inconsistencies and unpredicted events do arise, we are able to account for them by amending our rules and expectations about how the world behaves. This happens in everyday life as well as in science. Contrast this with the chaos and illogicality of what happens when we are dreaming.

A third argument is that recordings, both still (e.g. photographs) and moving (with or without audio reproduction) that are created by inanimate devices such as cameras, are immediately recognised by us as being what we ourselves perceive when we attend to 'the external world'.

An argument against the second possibility noted above, namely that reality is only what each person constructs for himself or herself, runs as follows. Suppose that two people, Ivan and Sonia, are stood together and they agree that they are both looking at some 'entity'. Is the 'entity' that Ivan is observing the same 'entity' that Sonia is observing? Does it exist in reality, separate from the two of them? The answer most people would give is yes, there exists some real, external entity or stimulus that affects both Ivan and Sonia; it gives rise to Ivan's experience and to Sonia's experience. Support for this assertion comes when measurements and other observations that Ivan and Sonia independently make about this entity concur—its agreed name (e.g. 'a car'), its colour and shape, its exact height, width and weight, and so on. This consistency encourages us to believe that the entity in question has an independent existence in 'the real world' separate from Sonia and Ivan; it is not something that only exists in each of their minds.

Working assumptions

Informed by the above deliberations, throughout the whole of our journey we shall adhere to certain core assumptions ('foundational beliefs') that we accept as givens, even though ultimately we cannot prove that they are 'the truth'. The first of these is as follows:

There is 'a real world', otherwise called 'reality', 'the objective world', 'the natural world' or 'Nature'[2], which exists without anyone observing it, although we, the observers, are all still part of it.

Despite this, we must forever be mindful that the only world any of us can know and speak of is 'the world we each experience in our head' or 'our subjective world', the world constructed by our brain from information coming through our senses.[3] We therefore need to recognise that:

How we perceive and describe the world that we individually and collectively construct is not equivalent to how the world is in reality.[4]

---

[2] Contrast the meaning of 'Nature', as used here, and 'nature' when we refer to the living world; for clarity, when I am using the term in the first sense I capitalise the first letter.

[3] The philosopher Immanuel Kant called this 'the phenomenal world' and reality 'the noumenal world'.

[4] It is legitimate to argue that the distinction 'real versus subjective world' is itself a construction of the subjective world. This poses no serious consequences for the road ahead.

Indeed, particularly in our modern era, we have come to understand that the world in reality differs in the most fundamental ways from the world represented by our minds. This greater understanding has come about through what some consider to be humanity's greatest ongoing intellectual achievement: science.[5] Hence our adherence to another important principle:

> *Continuously exploring the world that we experience through our senses brings us closer to understanding the true nature of the real world.[6] The best way we have of engaging in this process is thinking logically and rationally and adhering to science and the application of the scientific method.*

Consequently, whenever possible on our journey we shall take account of what science currently tells us is most likely to be true about the world. At least, nothing that we assume, assert or conclude should be contradicted by our current scientific understanding. For this reason, we shall encounter on our journey no references to or reliance on supernatural or religious propositions—God, gods or goddesses; ghosts and spirits; paranormal claims such as telepathy, thought transference and prophetic dreams; and so on.

An analogy

I am sure that I am not alone in finding philosophical debates about the meaning and nature of fundamentals such as

---

[5] One of the major reasons why science compels us to think of the world in ways that are radically different from what our everyday experience tells us is that by the application of technology (telescopes, microscopes, electromagnetic wave detectors, etc.) we are able to observe far more of our world than was previously possible through our unaided senses. This will prove an important consideration for further stages of our journey.

[6] Note the expression 'closer to understanding'. Maybe we shall never reach a *complete* understanding. Here the maths analogy of a convergent series may be apposite, though perhaps even this is over-idealistic.

knowledge, reality and existence difficult to keep up with, and one is apt to end up in a state of confusion. On such occasions, what may be helpful are analogies or metaphors from everyday life. For present purposes we can think of our mind's representation of the world as like a map of some territory (indeed we often use the term 'mental map'). The territory itself is akin to external reality. Different maps vary in how detailed and accurately they represent the territory but obviously, except in trivial ways, none of them bears any resemblance to the territory itself, hence the expression 'The map is not the territory'. Further discussion of this analogy may be found in Appendix I (but first see below).

Analogies are particularly useful when we need to change our way of thinking about some aspect of our world, in this case making an explicit distinction between our mind's representation of reality and reality itself.[7] On such occasions we can refer to how we usually think about some other aspect of the world (in the present case a map and the territory it represents). Even so, such analogies are still based on the mind's representation of reality. Consequently they are rarely, if ever, appropriate 100 per cent of the time. For example, we can only ever experience our mind's 'map' of reality whereas when we look at an actual map, we may also directly observe the territory it represents (strictly we should say 'the territory our mind represents'). Also, we do not consider that we ourselves, or indeed the map itself, are part of the territory (and neither are part of the map itself). In contrast, we and the mental maps we construct are always part of the real world. This point is worth stressing as follows:

Sentient beings, such as humans, are physical parts of the universe. Our structure and our functioning obey the same laws of nature as govern the rest of the universe.

---

[7] We may argue that we can only represent our world through metaphor or analogy—i.e. 'as if' ways of thinking. See Appendix I for further discussion around this.

More detailed analysis

The working assumptions that I have outlined above underpin all the arguments, reasoning, and conclusions that you will encounter as you proceed on this journey.

Now, you may be aware that what I have been discussing about reality and how our minds represent it constitutes a major part of philosophy, and for over 2000 years at least, this has been the subject of much debate amongst philosophers who still seem to be as divided as ever. If you imagine a spectrum of beliefs, on the extreme left being the dogma that reality is an illusion (more accurately a *delusion*) and all that exists is what your mind creates and, on the extreme right, the dogma that what your mind creates is a true reconstruction of the world in which you live, then our working assumptions lie somewhere between the two, probably closer to the right end.[8] I invite you to join me there if only for the purposes of this quest; even if you are reluctant to do so you will find that we are in good company (probably including most scientists) though there are plenty of people occupying positions either side of us.

Throughout our journey I shall be making constant reference to these working assumptions and the map analogy. In Appendix I, I present a more detailed exploration which you may find useful to study now or later (I would recommend later, say when you have reached the end of Part II of this book). I have used an appendix because at this stage I do not wish to burden you with too much information and analysis that is not essential for you to make sense of what is to come.

---

[8] Philosophers distinguish between *idealism*—there is no external reality, only the world constructed by the human mind—and *realism*, which accepts that there is a material world 'out there'. Realism may be *direct*—the world that we experience is the real world itself, and *indirect*, i.e. it is only a representation created by the brain. The position adopted here is closest to indirect realism.

The illusive 'I'

At this juncture, there is another important observation to note which we will repeatedly encounter on our journey: the way we think about our world, and the language we use to represent it, is replete with assumptions, inconsistencies and logical anomalies that we have no reason to believe are applicable to the objective world. Yet, paradoxically they arise from our representing the world in ways that best serve our needs and purposes. I shall illustrate this with what is, at this stage, an apposite example.

With a few possible exceptions, human beings may be the only creatures we know that can consciously reflect on themselves, i.e. experience an awareness of self. Although it may not be immediately apparent, this reveals itself at a basic level, as indicated when one says or thinks, 'I do X' meaning 'I am the agent of the activity X.' So you may say, 'I am running, walking, talking, sleeping, dreaming, remembering, eating, breathing, sweating' and so on. This also applies to your feelings and states of mind ('I am sad, angry, tired; 'I believe'; 'I'm not sure'); intentions ('I'll go and put the kettle on'); recollections ('I saw my friend yesterday'); activities you are not doing or did not do ('I never said that!'); or feelings you do not or did not have ('I'm not angry', 'I wasn't afraid').

Now, if you think deeply about these statements, a problem may seem to emerge. The problem is the elusive 'I'. Who, what or where is this 'I' that is responsible for or experiencing all these different activities or mental states?

The problem may become more obvious when we make explicit the reflective awareness inherent in these kinds of observations. First consider how you can make observations about someone else such as 'I am aware that she is running, she is going to put the kettle on, she is not feeling angry, she never said that', etc. In these instances there is a clear separation between 'I', the person who is aware, and the other person, 'she' whose behaviour or state of mind 'I' am aware of. Now consider the case where I think, 'I am aware that I am running, walking, talking, angry, not angry, about to go and put the kettle on, etc.'. Where now is the separation between the person who is aware (the first 'I') and the person who is running, walking, etc. (the second 'I')? And if you announce to the world, 'I am aware that I am running', which 'I' is making the announcement: the 'I' that is aware or the 'I' that is running? Indeed is there a third 'I', the one that is making this remark? (Maybe if, right now, you say aloud, 'I am aware that I am reading a book' it may help you understand the confusion here.)

The dilemma of 'the elusive I' becomes more apparent in more common examples of self-reflection such as 'I'm disappointed with myself', 'I decided to treat myself' and 'I know what I'm talking about' (and how about 'I said, "I'm not sure I know what I'm talking about"'?). Come to think of it, the same question arises when we say the same of other people, e.g. 'He's disappointed with himself.'

Now this discussion may seem to you more than a little frivolous. The 'problems' I have identified do not exist for us in our everyday life[9] and hence we have no need to feel we must set about solving them. But they do reveal limitations and contradictions in the ways our mind represents the world and how we communicate our experiences to others, and to ourselves. Hence we cannot accept that these ways provide us with accurate representations of the real world.

Throughout this book we shall encounter many such anomalies in the ways we have of understanding the world that make the most sense to us. When this happens, the procedure I adopt is as follows. First, I propose that there are no correct or incorrect answers to the questions that arise;

---

[9] Some writers may argue that this problem does indeed arise in certain unusual circumstances, such as the psychiatric condition multiple personality disorder (now termed dissociative identity disorder). I shall go no further than say that this is far too tendentious a diagnostic entity to reliably inform this discussion.

there *are* various answers, but their merits lie in how best they serve our everyday needs. These 'answers' are usually implicit and automatic in our thinking and behaviour—we are not even aware that any problems arise. But there are no *correct* answers. Moreover, 'correct' answers are not to be found in the real world either; that is, there are no experiments or observations that we can perform for this purpose (e.g. identifying 'the elusive I' above). We then need to think what might be a more realistic way of representing the world so that the anomalies don't arise at all and the questions just disappear.[10] As I noted earlier, this inevitably requires us to abandon our normal ways of thinking—the assumptions we implicitly make about our world—in favour of what often turns out to be a more simplified representation. But these representations themselves are still subjective: they can't be otherwise. All we can hope for is that *they more accurately represent reality*.

Meditation

'Why was I born the person I am?' 'Why am I me *(insert your name here)* and not someone else?' Having discussed the confusion that arises in the case of the illusive 'I', let's try to be clear about our terminology here. When, you ask yourself the above question you are implying a *duality*; there is 'I' on the one hand, who is aware of being 'me' on the other. This duality is evident in everyday life when we say things like, 'If I were Joe Biden, I wouldn't have pulled my troops out of Afghanistan.' By this we sometimes mean, 'If I were in Joe Biden's position, but we might also mean 'If I were really Joe Biden'. It is this literal interpretation of 'being someone else'

---

[10] Recall that in the Prologue I wondered if some of those fundamental questions I listed are 'based on a faulty understanding of our world, and when we think of the world in the correct way, the questions just go away'.

that is intended by the above question.[11] Indeed the 'I' here is more or less equivalent to how I defined the soul in the Prologue.

Now it may be that you have already rejected the notion that such a duality is tenable. I shall address this more fully in due course but for present purposes it need not be a problem. Think of it as an analogous or 'as if' way of speaking—it is *as if* there were a split between the person you are and your awareness of being that person.

I invite you now simply to consider the initial questions and ask yourself: 'If I had been born somebody else instead of the person I am, how would I or anybody else know? What detectable difference would there be?'

Once you have spent a little time thinking about this you will be ready to begin the journey in earnest.

---

[11] Of course, if you were 'really' Joe Biden you would do exactly as Joe Biden does!

PART II

CONSCIOUSNESS: THE HOST, THE
PERSON AND THE SOUL

CHAPTER 2

ABOUT CONSCIOUSNESS

Now that we have prepared the way, the first steps on our journey require us to spend some time thinking about what we mean by 'consciousness'. We shall then explore what we mean by our 'sense of self' and 'the person I am/you are' and discuss in more detail what in this book is intended by the term 'the soul'.

Thoughts on the nature of consciousness
The nature of consciousness presents one of the greatest challenges in science today and scientists are a long way from any credible answers. Perhaps this will always be the case and I am certainly not going to attempt any solutions or speculations about the essence of consciousness and what its underlying mechanisms may be; our search for answers to our questions does not require this. However, I shall insist that we adhere to the premise that all our conscious experiences require the activity of our brain. Moreover, I shall not be making any inferences to the effect that the material structure and functioning of the brain are insufficient to fully account for consciousness and that to

achieve this aim we must invoke some hypothetical and as yet undiscovered non-material entity. Some theorists consider that this is necessary, but I remain unconvinced.

Whatever the case, it seems clear to most people that consciousness is *of necessity* the result of brain activity. We can lose parts of our body, such as our limbs, and even suffer loss of function in parts of our nervous system, such as our spinal cord and sensory organs, but we can still be conscious, although what we can be conscious of is thus subject to restriction.

I have just used the expression 'conscious *of*'. I find it hard to think of being conscious but not being conscious of anything. We might try to physically eliminate all sensory stimulation—light, sound, touch, etc.—or train ourselves to ignore it; similarly, we may aim not to think about anything at all through some form of meditation. But if we succeed in doing this, if we are not conscious of anything, would we still be conscious? We can all agree that after a blow on the head or while under a general anaesthetic we would 'not be conscious of anything', but isn't there a difference between that experience (or 'non-experience', or being unconscious) and what we might achieve through meditation? In the latter case, we may still be conscious: conscious of being conscious of nothing. And being conscious of that! None of this would be possible after being knocked out.

Meditation

Perhaps it will help us if we just think about what kinds of things we are conscious of. I therefore invite you, before proceeding, to consider this question simply by observing the kinds of things of which you are aware. Do they fall into different categories, or types of experiences?

---0---

The sense of self or personal identity
It seems that there are indeed various areas of conscious experience. The ones that I am thinking of are:

1. Awareness of stimuli and events in the outside world as detected by our senses—predominantly sight, sound, touch, taste, and smell.

2. Awareness of activities and processes going on in our bodies, such as aches and pains, digestive activity, breathing, positions and movements of body parts, and tiredness.

3. Awareness of activity originating in our brain (our mind)—thoughts, images, memories, dreams, etc.

Most conscious experience consists of combinations of the above, as when we respond emotionally to some external event. (Arguably, the act of dreaming, for example, and some profound meditative states involve awareness almost exclusively of mental activity.)

In addition to the above, or more plausibly as an extension of the third type of consciousness, there is one specific sort of 'awareness of something' that is difficult to capture in words although we have already discussed it in the Prologue and chapter 1. It is commonly referred to as 'the sense of self', or 'awareness of being', the ability to reflect on awareness of being the individual who is having these conscious experiences. In other words, these experiences 'belong' to an individual, i.e. the person *you* are.

Imagine that you are listening to one of your favourite pieces of music. You are conscious of the music and your emotional reaction to it. You are also *aware of being conscious* of these things, of being the individual who is experiencing the music at that particular time and who feels the associated emotions. You can think to yourself (although I'm guessing you wouldn't!) 'The person I am is listening to and enjoying this music' just as someone observing you can think, *'That person* is listening to and enjoying the music.'

Also, for you and the above observer, the person who is having these experiences at any given moment is the same

27

person *at any other moment* during this activity. That is, with each new conscious sensation there isn't a different person that experiences it; you remain that same person. Moreover this 'same person' extends over your lifetime. For example, while listening to the music, you may recall the first time you heard it—say at a party with some friends when you were years younger. For you and anyone else, that person hearing the music for the first time is *the same person* who is hearing it now; he or she is not a different person from *you now* in the way you would think, say, a friend who was also at the party listening to the same music is a different person from you[12]. This is not just an assumption you make; it is how you experience life. You are always aware of having been, and of still being, that same person you were in the past, even as you are thinking of it (the memory) from an outside perspective.

Similarly, while you are listening to the music now, you may think that the next time the opportunity presents itself you will attend a live performance by the same band. You are now conscious of a pleasant feeling of anticipation as you make your decision. There is no doubt in your mind that the person whom you imagine having this enjoyable experience in the future is the same person who is having this enjoyable experience now and the same person who had this experience in the past. Moreover, the 'I' that is aware of being that person now (you) and in the past will also be the 'I' that will experience being that person when he or she goes to the concert. Indeed, this will be confirmed for you when the event actually happens; you may look back and recall this occasion that you decided you would like to see the band again, along with your eager anticipation when doing so.

I hope this conveys what I mean by the awareness or sense of self or personal identity, something that is more than

---

[12] You may of course say, 'I'm not the same person as I was then', in the sense that your personality has changed a lot in the meantime, but this is not the meaning intended here.

being conscious. It is something that extends over a person's lifetime and enables us to ask those fundamental questions such as 'Why was I born the person I am and not somebody else?' 'When I die, will I be reincarnated as someone else?' In other words, it is what we are, for our purposes, defining as the soul.

Now it may be that a few questions and problems about all of this have already occurred to you. Indeed this business of the apparent continuity of personal identity over time is one that we shall need to return to and study in greater depth later in our journey. For the moment, you are entitled to remain sceptical about the distinction that I have created between 'I' and the person 'I' am. I simply ask you to bear with me for a while and see where it takes us.

One more thing to consider about consciousness is that both in qualitative and quantitative terms, consciousness is not an all-or-nothing phenomenon. Firstly, in simple terms we can talk about our level of consciousness at any particular time, albeit with qualitative variations. We may be in a state of non-dream sleep, dream sleep, intoxication, concussion, drowsiness, and so on, or be 'wide awake'. Some people may also suffer a brain injury that affects their level of consciousness or restricts it in significant ways.

Secondly, it is a possible that there are species on our planet other than *homo sapiens* that experience consciousness but in a more limited manner, depending on the size and complexity of their brains. (The same may also apply to what I refer to above as 'the sense of self'.) In addition there may come a time when scientists can build intelligent machines that are of such complexity that they are capable of some degree of consciousness.

This is an apposite moment to note that throughout this book I sometimes use the term 'conscious' (and 'consciousness') and sometimes 'aware' (and 'awareness'). Is there any difference? I must confess that the reasons for my selective use of these terms are decidedly fuzzy. When I use the term 'aware' I am thinking about the basic level of awareness of which most, if not all, species of animal are capable. I tend to use the term 'conscious' when I am thinking of awareness as experienced by human beings and, to a lesser degree, maybe by other animals high in the phylogenetic scale, and this includes self-awareness or self-reflection. I am not very strict about this distinction, but I do try to avoid any confusion where this may arise.

Meditation

I invite you now to continue to think deeply about those two questions 'Why was I born the person I am?' and 'Why am I *me* and not someone else?' In the Prologue of this book I asked you to consider whether these questions have any real meaning for you. For me personally, they do. Indeed they feel like very profound questions. But I have noticed something very interesting; I can only ask these questions *of myself*. If I look at another person and ask, 'Why was she born the person she is and not somebody else?' then none of these questions seem to have any meaning. It would seem *to me* to make no difference at all if you or he or she or anyone at all *except me* were indeed born as someone else (so long as the person they actually are still exists). I wonder if you have the same reaction as me.

CHAPTER 3

DEFINING THE HOST, THE PERSON AND THE SOUL

In this chapter I shall continue the discussion in the preceding chapter by introducing a tripartite model that applies to any individual human being. Before I describe the three parts, I issue a warning: beware distinctions! Distinctions are ways the human mind represents and communicates about the world to other minds. As such, they may not (you may say they *do not*) represent the world in reality. Hence, what I am about to describe is a *working model*, a set of assumptions that will allow us to advance our exploration of the questions we are addressing, but which eventually we will have to modify or replace as its limitations become more manifest.

The working model represents any human being in terms of three constructs: Host, Person and Soul. So far, I have indicated that 'Soul' is your awareness of being the unique individual, i.e. the 'Person', you are. Notice the initial capital letter of each, which denotes that they are being used in these defined ways. When they are not, I shall revert to the usual lower case.

Let's explore a little further the meaning of Soul. To repeat, it is your 'awareness of being' and this is restricted to awareness of being the person *you* are, awareness of experiencing what *you* are experiencing, awareness of doing what *you* are doing, awareness of feeling what *you* are feeling, awareness of thinking what *you* are thinking, and so on. It also includes, under normal circumstances, awareness of the experience of always having been *you* in your past, and awareness of the anticipation of always being *that person* in the future. It is the 'I' in the questions 'Why am I the person I am?' and 'Why was I born *this* person and not someone else?' So let 'Soul [You]' refer to your Soul, Soul [Me] to my Soul, Soul [Maria] to Maria's Soul, and so on.

It is important to note here that the Soul is essentially 'mere awareness'. The Soul does not engage in what psychologists call 'executive functions', such as controlling the content of consciousness, directing activity, or deciding what to do at any time.[13]

To repeat, our second construct: Person [You], is the unique individual *(insert your name her)* that Soul [You] is aware

---

[13] Some philosophers and neuroscientists might equate what I have defined as the Soul with consciousness itself. For them, consciousness is indeed like a passive observer and, contrary to what we normally experience, does not control, direct or influence our behaviour and experience in any way. Thus Oakley & Halligan (2017) state, 'In this sense, personal awareness is analogous to the rainbow which accompanies physical processes in the atmosphere but exerts no influence over them.' For present purposes we can get by without accepting or rejecting such ideas, although they are ultimately of great importance. (We shall see in due course that it is more accurate to think of the Soul as an activity, something the brain does, rather than some 'thing'. As such, I believe it must have the potential to have some influence on other brain activity and, therefore, events in the surrounding environment. However, it is best for present purposes to think of the Soul as being like a passive observer.)

of being. I shall describe in greater detail what 'Person' refers to in due course.

There is one more distinction to make here: this is what I shall call a 'Host'. A Host is a physical, functioning entity that is capable of being a Person and 'having a Soul'. In your case it is the *physical* you—Host [You]—the product of your unique genetic endowment (the base pair sequence in DNA), as with any other person. Effectively, most of the time I use this term, it will be with particular reference to the brain and nervous system of the person concerned.

You may recall that in chapter 1 I discussed the 'the elusive I' and suggested that the questions raised by this have no answers, as the problem lies in how we subjectively represent our world. So I need to emphasise that this tripartite working model is not my attempt to provide any answers to this conundrum.

As things stand at the moment, how does our working model address the principal question, 'What happens to me when I die?' Obviously, death means that Host [You] ceases to function and therefore to exist, and likewise Person [You] must also cease to exist. What becomes of Soul [You]? Obviously, when you die it can't be Soul [You] anymore, since Host [You] and Person [You] no longer exist. We then ask, for example, does it 'become' Soul [Someone Else]? It seems that at this stage our conclusion must be that when the Host dies, the Person dies, and so too must his or her Soul.

And thus we have answered our questions! Or have we?

Meditation

I invite you now to consider this well-known thought experiment. You may have sometimes said about someone else, 'I wish I were him (or her)', probably because you envy that person in some way. By this you mean changing your whole identity to become that person, leaving behind the person you are.

Right now I invite you to think of one of your friends. Imagine that just for one whole minute you are going to change identities with your friend. You are going to become your friend and he or she is going to become you, but just for that one minute. Then you will switch back again. In other words, you are going to exchange Souls just for a minute. I encourage you to give this some thought before reading on.

The underlying question is this: How would you know that the exercise has been successful or not? How would you know that, for one minute, you became your friend, and your friend became you?

CHAPTER 4

MORE ABOUT THE SOUL

Let's start by considering the meditation at the end of the previous chapter. I have found that people are quite able to understand and participate in this little exercise but give different responses to the questions asked. The main purpose here is not to discover what the correct answer is, though most likely your answer will be that somehow you know that you did not become your friend and *vice versa*. But if you *had* switched, what would there be to notice? Once you became your friend, for that whole minute you would have all the experience of being him or her and no memories beyond his or hers. There would be absolutely no detectable difference in that person's experience had you not become him or her. And the same argument would apply in the case of your friend becoming you.

If you *did* switch, once you switched back what would you now recall about that minute? Since your memories belong to the person you are, then you are not going to remember anything different than if you did switch. You will not retain the memories of being your friend and neither will your friend retain the memories of being *you*. Your brain will only recall the memories of being *you* during that minute, similarly your friend. So, whether you switched or not, you would both deny having done so![14]

So maybe the questions we have asked, notably 'Why am I the person I am and not somebody else?' *are* meaningless. Maybe they are as meaningless as asking, say, 'Why is the computer in front of me not the television over there and *vice versa*?' or thinking about whether it's possible for the computer to become the television for one minute and the television to become the computer. The computer is the computer, and the television is the television, and that's all there is to it!

If this is correct, then the mistake we have made is to create a duality where none exists. The duality, in this case, is *the person you are* and *your awareness of being that person* (Person [You] versus Soul [You]). The other, more common duality is *the person you are* and *your physical body*—Person [You] versus Host [You]. It's important that we examine both of these dualities further as they have the potential to lead us seriously astray on our journey. In both cases I shall make the point that they are useful *distinctions* for our everyday purposes but not necessarily *dualities* that exist in reality.

Consider the distinction Person and Soul. Some religious and quasi-religious beliefs hold that when you die you are reincarnated as another being—a person or even an animal—though unaware of being the person you were in your previous life. Such beliefs, which are not uncommon, require that the Soul can be separated from the person you

---

[14] We can extend this to the fantasy that every day of your life you wake up as a different person. Following the same reasoning as in the exercise described, you would have no way of knowing whether or not this is the case. Yet most people feel that somehow they *know* that this is not the case and that they have always been the person they are.

are and is somehow free to be transferred to other minds. [15] This was the assumption behind the meditation in which you imagined becoming your friend and *vice versa*. All of this is inconsistent with current scientific knowledge about the human mind and brain; hence the idea of detachment of Soul and Person must be rejected,[16] along with religious and supernatural beliefs based upon it. Despite this, although we should be mindful of its limitations, the distinction *the person you are* and *your awareness of being that person* does have some kind of validity; it makes sense to most people, as has already been illustrated, and is of central importance for our journey.[17]

Now consider the second duality *the person you are* and your *physical body*, including your nervous system (commonly referred to as mind-body dualism). This is central to many religious faiths, most notably in relation to one's fate after death; our body is destroyed but our soul (this time meaning the person we are and, presumably, our self-awareness) is preserved and, for example, in the Christian and Muslim faiths, is received into Heaven or Hell according to how we

---

[15] It seems that this kind of reincarnation requires that we each have a Soul in the sense of 'awareness of being'. Would it make any sense to believe that human beings are reincarnated as trees for example and *vice versa*? This would require trees to be capable of awareness of being, and that is most unlikely!

[16] Even some scientists may disagree with this but the evidence that people in some way have memories of previous existences or can be hypnotically regressed to their 'past lives' is not, in my opinion, persuasive.

[17] The distinction has some support from consideration of the neurological basis of conscious experience, as revealed by types of brain malfunctioning such as certain forms of epilepsy in which consciousness appears to be preserved but not the sense of self (Damasio, 2000). It is also similar to the distinction made in cognitive psychology between first- and second-order thinking (Rosenthal, 2005).

have led our lives. Other faiths hold that, having died, we continue our survival 'on the other side' in the spirit world and can even, in our spirit form, revisit those we have 'left behind' and communicate with them. Once more, these ideas are inconsistent with current scientific knowledge about the human mind and brain and hence *this* duality—the idea of separation of mind and body—must also be rejected[18] along with religious and supernatural beliefs based upon it. Again, however, the mind-body *distinction* is one that people can understand and, for present purposes it has considerable utility. I shall say more about this in due course.

---

[18] There are scientists who are committed to such beliefs because of their religion. Some scientists also accept the mind-body duality by citing evidence from investigations of out-of-body and near-death experiences. Again I remain sceptical.

CHAPTER 5

MORE ABOUT THE HOST

Recall the distinctions I have been making: Host [You], Person [You] and Soul [You]. As I have said, a Host is a functioning individual being in his or her physical form. Hence, when I speak of a Host, I am being absolutely materialistic; a Host is a collection of matter that is so structured that it is capable of being conscious and aware of its own existence—of 'being a Person' and 'having a Soul'. As already noted, at this stage these distinctions are being described very much in terms of 'the world as it seems to us' rather 'than the world as it is in reality'. How are they to be understood from the latter standpoint? Our aim should be to come closer to answering this question. So let's examine them in more detail, starting with the Host.

Just for simplicity, let's first work on the assumption that the only Hosts in the universe are human beings on planet Earth. A Host, thus described, is the entire body of an individual human being, but when we are considering the capability of experiencing consciousness and awareness of being, we usually assume this to be a property of the nervous system, and in particular, the brain. Let's therefore consider in more detail what science has discovered about the human nervous system.

The human nervous system

The human nervous system consists of billions of tiny cells made from complex proteins. There are two main types of cells—neurons and glia. Most neurons consist of a cell body, a bush of fibres called dendrites, and an axon. Neurons 'fire'—that is, they communicate with each other—typically by the transmission of a kind of electrical impulse from the cell body along the length of the axon, which is picked up by the cell bodies or dendrites of adjacent neurons. The impulse may then be transmitted to ('excite') another nerve cell—this is going on all the time in billions of nerve cells in your brain—or the impulse may inhibit another neuron from 'firing' in this way.

The impulse that travels down the axon consists of a wave of positive charges that is created by minute electrically charged particles called ions moving through the neuron membrane. This wave reaches the axon terminals at a region called the synapse, where it may cross the tiny gap (the synaptic cleft) to excite or inhibit adjacent neurons. However, in most cases, the message is conveyed by the release of chemicals called neurotransmitters that move across the synaptic cleft, most often from several synapses simultaneously. What happens at the synapses—those miniscule junctions between trillions of nerve endings—dictates much of human experience and behaviour and what may go wrong with both.

Neurons fire when the potential difference created by the flow of ions exceeds a certain value called the action potential; thus, either the impulse is conveyed or it is not. The actual strength of a nerve impulse is related to the numerical frequency of the action potentials.

It is estimated that there are over 80 billion neurons in the human brain and that each neuron has an average of seven thousand synaptic connections to other neurons. There are many more glial cells than neurons; these support, protect, nourish and insulate the neurons but they are also believed to play a part in information processing.

Reasons to be astonished

Let's pause here to consider two perspectives about which I never fail to be astonished. Firstly, the above description of the nervous system leads us to the conclusion that any activity we humans engage in requires, at some stage, precisely coordinated, tiny movements of trillions of minute particles in and between billions of tiny nerve cells in our body. We can imagine what is happening at the same level when that activity involves the coordinated efforts of several people, even hundreds and thousands of people. This applies not merely to the mundane activities of daily life, but to the great achievements of any human being—scientist, writer, painter, composer, sportsperson, political leader and, seriously, yourself—as well as human beings working together on huge enterprises that have changed our world and our lives.[19]

Secondly, let us put the Host in context. For most of our history we believed that we Earthlings were the centre of the universe, even the sole reason for its existence. But no longer. Now, when we think of the universe, we imagine billions of galaxies each containing billions of stars. We know that many stars have a planet or planets in orbit around them, just as in our own solar system. On some of those planets, which will be tiny in comparison to their suns, there may be forms of life, but it is likely that conditions that support life only exist on a small proportion of planets. On some of these, again

---

[19]There is an argument for maintaining that *any* activity of *anything* in the universe involves, at some stage, activity at the microscopic level (see later chapters) but this does not make me any the less astonished.

probably a small minority, there will be forms of life—Hosts—that are conscious and self-aware. Hence, Hosts comprise an indescribably tiny proportion of the known universe.

Biologists often play down any suggestion that there is something particularly special about human beings, or that they represent some significant stage or end point in the evolutionary process in general. Evolution is not a process that is designed to create conscious, intelligent beings; successful evolution is to do with how a species, over generations, adapts to its environment to maximise its survival potential. Thus the significance of consciousness is likely to be its survival value for the species, just as having horns on the head, fur on the body, a tail at the end of the body, etc., has survival value for members of other species. Also, scientists tell us that we should be cautious about describing anything in the universe as 'remarkable', 'extraordinary', or 'special', as these qualities only exist in our subjective ways of categorising and judging things.

We can accept all of this, but is there not a different point of view? It has taken billions of years for conditions in the universe to evolve to enable planets to form, and for conditions on planets to be present—and present for long enough—for matter to combine and develop in such a way that it has the property of life, and more billions of years to have the capability of being conscious and self-aware, i.e. to be a Host. And isn't it valid to say that these extremely rare and minute bits of the universe, in the form of the human brain, are possibly the most extraordinary and complex things in the universe? Doesn't that in itself make our planet a very special place?

I therefore invite you to think of yourself and the universe from these perspectives. When we are close to the end of our journey I shall argue that, while maintaining a materialistic stance, and without having to accept any religious or transcendental notions about our origins or purpose. it is still valid to consider Hosts, those intelligent forms of life such as human beings, as being of special significance in our universe's development. But we still have a lot more work to do before then.

CHAPTER 6

MORE ABOUT THE PERSON

In this chapter I shall explore with you a very important way of thinking about consciousness and what we have identified as the Host, the Person, and the Soul. It may seem a very simple point that I am making, but it is absolutely central and will stand us in good stead on our travels. Should we go astray it will prove to be a useful compass to set us back on the right pathway.

By way of preparation, may I ask you to do something rather silly? Please give a wave with your right arm now. Keep the wave going for a moment.

Now for the first question: What sort of wave is it? Is it an energetic wave? A reluctant wave? Perhaps even a regal wave? You may relax now.

My next questions are 'What has happened to the wave now?' and 'Where has it gone?' I imagine your reply is something like, 'The wave hasn't "gone" anywhere. I have simply stopped waving.'

Now may I ask you to wave again in the same manner as you did just now? My question this time is, 'Is this the same wave as before?' I imagine that now you hesitate a little before you decide on your reply, but if you have followed my instructions, your answer will probably be yes. I then ask you, 'If this is the same wave, what happened to it when you stopped waving just now? Where did it go, and where has it come back from?' Again, with commendable patience, you will probably reply that the wave did not go anywhere. Maybe to clarify matters you say something like, 'I was just waving in the same way as the first time.'

So what is the important principle that all this is leading to? In a nutshell, it is as follows: It is important *at this stage of our journey* that we make a clear distinction between objects (in the above example, your arm) and the activity of those objects—what they do (in this case 'wave'). We must be especially careful to do this when considering conscious experience and the Host, Person, and Soul.[20]

Thus, in the above exercise we should think of your arm is an object, and the wave as an *activity* of the arm: it's what your arm *does*. So when you stop waving, the wave does not go anywhere. You can resume waving in a similar manner, but the wave is not 'the same wave' as before in the sense that we would say the arm that is waving is 'the same arm'.

This goes for any activity of the body. A 'kick' is what our leg *does*; a 'punch' is what our hand *does*; a 'nod' is what our head *does*; and so on. But none of these activities exist as entities. *And this equally applies to whatever our brain does.*

Let's consider one activity of our brain: remembering. For a moment could I ask you now to bring to mind a childhood

---

[20] In line with what we discussed in chapter 1, one could argue that this distinction between objects and what they do—i.e. the activity they engage in—is one that sentient beings like humans impose upon the world rather than a property of the world itself. Indeed, we shall later have to explore this matter more thoroughly. However, I do not believe that this alters the validity of arguments based upon this distinction in the present context, where the 'objects' are human beings or their constituent parts, and their activities are governed by the brain and nervous system.

memory? Just as in the example of waving, I could ask you what sort of memory it is (sad, happy, exciting, etc.) and you would have little difficulty understanding me and replying. When you stop thinking of this memory and I ask you, 'What has happened to the memory?' and 'Where has it gone?' you may reply, as before, 'It hasn't gone anywhere, I've just stopped thinking about it.' If I ask you to think about the memory a second time and then ask you, 'Is it the same memory as before?' you would have no difficulty in saying that it is. But, once again, just as in the case of a wave of the arm, it is not that the memory exists somewhere and 'comes back' when we recall it. We certainly talk about memories as though they are like this, but the reality is that there are no such *things* as memories. They do not exist as corporeal entities. We do not really *have* memories, in the way we *have* a computer, a car, a watch, or our body parts.

Now it may be argued that there are parts of the brain where memories are 'stored', and that damaging these areas impairs or prevents the storage of memories and their retrieval, i.e. recall. However, we can only say that this is so *in a manner of speaking*. When we recall a previous event, it is not simply the case that a memory is stored in a particular neural network and on recall it is released into consciousness in a way similar to drawing a file from a filing cabinet or finding a photograph in an album. Remembering is a constructive *activity* involving diverse parts of the brain, not just one memory store, 'file' or 'bank'. For example, after setting down this book you may think about some the things discussed in this chapter. To enable you to do that, the act of reading this information at this very moment is bringing about structural changes in certain parts of your brain. These changes, if they persist, will allow your brain to *engage in the activity* of recalling the information at a later time. The same may be said of longer-term memories, such as what you did on your last holiday, how you celebrated your sixteenth birthday, or what happened on your first day at school.

We can go further with this and say that there are no such entities as *thoughts*: Our brain is structured to enable us to engage in the *activity* of thinking. There are no such *things* as images: we *imagine*. There are no such *things* as perceptions: we *perceive*. We do not *have* a dream: we dream. And, just as we said of activities such as waving, punching, and kicking, as well as remembering, when we stop thinking, the thought does not still exist somewhere; when we stop imagining, the image does not exist somewhere—it never 'exists' at all; likewise when we stop perceiving, dreaming, and so on.

Thus our mind is not something that we *have*; it is an activity that our brain *does*! In chapter 5 it was noted that our brain consists of billions of nerve cells, and that the total number of interconnections between them is in the order of trillions. This permits an incomprehensible number of patterns of interaction over an interval of time, especially given the fact that any one nerve cell may be involved more than once in a circuit of activity. We can reasonably suggest that it is the sheer scale and complexity of these interconnections that enable the Host, unlike all other known physical entities, to have the property of consciousness, in the way that we have defined consciousness: that is, to 'have a mind'. But it must always be remembered that there is no such thing or entity as 'the mind'. Likewise, there is no such *thing* as 'the conscious mind' or 'the unconscious mind'. There is brain activity that is consciously experienced or not consciously experienced (or, more likely, there is a continuum in this respect). What we humans experience as our 'mind' is the activity of our brain, what our brain *is doing*.

It is now just a simple logical step to extend this way of thinking to the concept of Host and Person. According to our understanding of these terms, *the Person is an activity of the Host. It is what the Host does.* **You are an activity!** It is therefore possible to state, 'I do, therefore I am.'[21] In this way, there is no real Person-Host duality in the same sense as the traditional mind-body duality that philosophers and psychologists have long fought over.

It is also clear that the Soul itself—the awareness of being—is not a thing or entity, although it is much more convenient to talk about it in this way. It is an activity of the brain; or, just as in the case of the Person, we can say the Soul is an activity of the Host, something the Host does. Indeed, we may say that the Host engages in the activity of 'the Person', which includes the activity 'awareness of being'— i.e. 'the Soul'. Hence, from this standpoint, there is really no Person-Soul duality either; that is, there is no actual separation of being a person and being aware of being that person.[22]

There is another important implication of our conclusions, one that should be made explicit. We have been speaking of 'two worlds', one the real world and the other the subjective world, as if they are *both* entities. Now we see that—again more realistically—the subjective world is not an entity: it is an activity performed by our brains.

---

[21] The more common expression, attributed to the French philosopher René Descartes, is of course 'I think, therefore I am.' The statement 'I do therefore I am' is not so different if one accepts that an alternative translation of Descartes' maxim 'Je pense donc je suis' is 'I *am thinking*, therefore I am.'

[22] Throughout this book I shall still refer, in the usual way, to various activities as if they are entities so long as it is not misleading to do so; the alternative leads to some very convoluted expressions which I wish to avoid! For example, if we take the idea 'the Host does the Person' into everyday life then we would have to alter some of the ways we address people. If you were confronted, say, by someone who looks like Joe Biden, instead of saying, 'Excuse me, are you Joe Biden?' you might say, 'Excuse me, are you the object that is doing Joe Biden?'!

Implications

Does any of this help us to move away from our default position, adopted at the outset, on the fate of the Soul? I have stated that our being is in our doing. Perhaps, therefore, it is more accurate to say that, rather than our awareness of *being*, the Soul is our awareness of *doing*—awareness of thinking, imagining, remembering, and so on. Whatever the case, when we stop doing, we stop being. When all activity in the brain or any other entity capable of consciousness ceases, the individual ceases to be.

Putting all of this in our present terminology, we can say that when Host [You] stops functioning—when you die—Host [You] can no longer *do* Person [You] and Soul [You]; therefore Person [You] and Soul [You] cease to exist. Death means oblivion

So we still find ourselves with the conclusion expressed at the end of chapter 3: death is oblivion for us all! But we still have a long way to go.

Meditation

If death means oblivion, then it must follow that before Host [You] existed, there was oblivion also. So, if you had not been born the Host you are now, you would not have been born at all. *All* would be oblivion, as far as you are concerned.

Now, if we accept this conclusion, then we must confront what, at least at first, seems to be a very strange consequence. In fact this is something that we will encounter more than once on our journey. It is the idea that for something to exist or take place, a myriad of other conditions, some of them extremely precise, must also be, or have been, in place. A common remark in the face of all this is, 'It's too much of a coincidence.'

The following is a meditation on this theme. I invite you to think about all the different things that needed to have happened, or to have been in place, to enable you (here we mean Host [You]) to have been born. What could have happened to prevent this? Some conditions were listed in the Prologue, such as your parents never having met, their deciding to have no more children before you were conceived, or a different sperm fertilising your mother's egg. But there are many, many more!

CHAPTER 7

THE UNLIKELINESS OF ME

As I came into the building just now, I noticed a car with the number plate XE12 RBS. Isn't that astonishing? Of all the millions of registration numbers it could have been, it turned out to be that one!

—attributed (with some modification) to Michael Shermer

I call the meditation at the end of the last section 'the unlikeliness of me'. We shall discover in due course that this is a recurrent and important theme, so we shall explore it in some depth. At this stage it has very much to do with our understanding of Soul as I have defined it here.

Thoughts on reincarnation
Consider one unique Host and the Person it 'does', namely John Smith, born at 10:07 p.m. on May 4, 1919, died at 1:27 p.m. on August 19, 2003. While he was alive, John asked himself the kind of questions that we listed in the Prologue. In particular he asked, 'Why was I born John Smith and not someone else?' and 'What will happen to me when I die?' He acknowledged the fact that his identity as John Smith ceases

at his death. He did not accept any religious teachings about meeting his creator in Heaven or going to Hell and saw no reason to believe that he would be encountering his deceased relatives, friends and acquaintances 'on the other side'. He therefore concluded that either death means oblivion, or that after his death he would be reincarnated as another sentient being yet to be born, let's say Tom Green. However if he continued thinking rationally about the latter outcome it is likely that he would reject it. Let us try to understand why.

When considering this possibility, John was making the Person-Soul distinction that we have already examined.[23] His Soul is his 'awareness of being' and in his present life he is aware of being Person [John]. When Host [John] dies, and with it Person [John], in the reincarnation scenario 'he' then becomes aware of being Person [Tom]. Thus Soul [John] and Soul [Tom] are in effect 'the same Soul'.[24]

One problem with John being reincarnated as Tom is that we are left with another question 'Why Tom and not someone else?' And there is another problem with this idea of reincarnation whereby we have past and future lives. If we go back in time we get into great difficulties to do with the number of Souls and the number of available Hosts and whether these numbers are compatible. As the Earth's population has increased so much over time, they aren't compatible, unless some people have 'new' Souls that have not been previously attached to any previous individual.

In fact, this simple idea of previous and future incarnations lacks any rational basis or any reason why it should be the case in reality.

---

[23] In fact he was engaging in dualism, something that we have already foresworn. However this is not the reason why he himself rejected the idea of reincarnation, as we shall see.

[24] Of course, if what we are considering were the case, Person [Tom] would have absolutely no awareness of his Soul having once been Soul [John]. I have earlier expressed doubts about the validity of claims by certain people that they are able to recall previous lives.

Now put yourself in John's position. You have concluded that you never experienced awareness before you were born. Only while you are alive do you experience awareness (i.e. of being the person you are). And when you die you will never experience awareness again. Thus 'awareness of being' appears to be locked into the person one is currently aware of being! So now you must tell yourself, 'If something had happened to stop me being born, I would have lost the chance of experiencing being any person at all, or any kind of conscious entity.' It is as though—*very much in a manner of speaking*—each one of us had only one opportunity of being a conscious entity, and that is as the person we are.[25]

Putting it this way, it does seem that you would have lost the chance of experiencing being *any person* if your parents had never met (likewise your grandparents, great grandparents, etc.), or your parents had decided to have no more children before you were conceived, and so on.

What about if a different sperm had fertilised the original egg? Let's remind ourselves that, ignoring artificial means of conception, every individual originates, during intercourse, from one unique sperm, out of around 100 million, that fertilises a single egg. The individual's unique genetic constitution is thus established, and an environment is in place (the mother's womb) for the fertilised egg to develop over the course of around nine months into a baby ready to be born and live in physical separation from its mother.

If a *different* sperm succeeded in fertilising the egg, then a genetically different individual would have been created (maybe of the opposite sex) but would you now be

---

[25] One answer might be that if you hadn't been born the person you are now, you would have been born as someone else. So, in the case of John Smith, he might have been born as, say, Mary Jones. In other words, what would have been Soul [John] would be Soul [Mary] instead. But then we would ask, 'Why Mary Jones'? and 'What would happen to Soul [Mary] that would have existed had John Smith *actually* been born?' So really we are no further forward.

experiencing being that person? There's no way of knowing this but it seems unlikely. It's possible in the same act of intercourse for two different sperm cells to fertilise two different eggs, in which case fraternal twins are created, each with their own Souls (as with non-twin siblings, originating from different acts of intercourse). In fact we have the same outcome when *one* sperm cell fertilises *one* egg and identical twins are produced by splitting of the fertilised egg.

So it seems that you owe your existence as a sentient being to a unique sperm-egg pairing. Since up to the present there must have existed countless trillions of sperm cells and trillions of egg cells, the possible number of unique individuals that *could* have existed is unimaginably huge. Of course, the vast majority could not have been conceived because, for one thing, in only a small fraction of sperm-egg pairings would their time periods of viability overlap. [26]

To recap: the premise that we are examining here is that a specific sperm cell combined with a specific egg produces a unique individual, and each individual is associated with a unique Soul. If we take this to its logical conclusion, then it follows that the overwhelming majority of potential individuals never have the chance of existing, and, crucially, *neither do the Souls associated with them.* As Richard Dawkins (1998) puts it: 'Most people are never going to die because they are never going to be born. The potential people who could have been here in my place but who will in fact never see the light of day outnumber the sand grains of Arabia.'

So, according to this theory, the answer to John Smith's question 'Would I have lost the chance of experiencing being a person if a different sperm had fertilised the egg?' is yes.

---

[26] It is possible to go down the road of assuming that Host and Soul are just defined by the egg, regardless of the fertilising sperm. I am not going to do this, and, in any case, the outcome of the argument is the same as if a unique *sperm-egg pairing* is assumed to underlie the Host's identity.

Host [John] would never have existed and if Soul [John] is uniquely integral to and dependent on Host [John], Soul [John] would never have existed either.

From this, John would probably consider that he was extraordinarily lucky to have been born at all, and thus to experience 'awareness of being'! And the same goes for you. Recall the meditation in the last chapter, namely to think of all the different things that could have happened to stop you being born. Not only did the sperm that originally fertilised the egg compete with millions of other sperms, but you also had to make it through those nine months in the womb. What if your parents had never met in the first place? Think of all the actions and decisions that each of them had to take that led them to meet and to decide to form a relationship. Now apply this thinking to *their* parents. And to *their* parents, and so on. If we are asserting that each person, each unique Host with its unique Soul, is the product of a unique sperm and a unique egg, then it seems to be remarkable that *that* sperm and *that* egg were created in the first place.

The unlikeliness of anything
One rejoinder to this puzzle is to say that the only way you can be astonished that all the circumstances necessary for your existence are in place is for them to *be* in place. If they weren't, then you wouldn't be alive to be astonished at the improbability of your existence!

Another way of looking at all of this is as follows: *any* thing that you can point to or *any* event that has occurred owes its presence or occurrence to such an unfathomable number of factors or antecedents that it seems so unlikely. For example, how did those shoes that you are now wearing come to be in the exact location they are in at this particular moment? Once you start thinking about this, your thoughts will take you further and further back in time, and, rather like a family tree, more and more conditions will need to have been in place for the final outcome, namely those particular shoes being in existence and being at that exact location right now. Isn't any single thing or event so extraordinarily unlikely? In fact, we can call this argument 'the unlikeliness of *anything*'.

All in all, arguments against a particular idea that proceed along the lines 'What would have happened to Y if X hadn't happened' (counterfactuals, as they are known) are not very convincing. For example (and this is another recurring theme on our journey), for X *not* to have happened requires other circumstances to have been different, and in order for *those* circumstances to have been different yet more circumstances would have had to be different, and so on and on. Hence we might as well say that X and Y occur in reality because that's the way reality has turned out,[27] and any other outcome would have been just as unlikely.

To drive home this point, let's consider the following. You toss an unbiased coin one hundred times and you are astonished to land one hundred heads. Yet a run of one hundred heads is just as likely as any other sequence you could obtain. Hence you could argue you should be astonished by *any* sequence of heads and tails.[28]

Let me tell you where I stand on this. That the physical person I am exists at all (i.e. Host [Me] and its activity, Person [Me]) isn't something for me to be so astonished about. Yes, I am only one of trillions upon trillions of possible combinations of DNA, genes, atoms or whatever that could exist as a human being, and the overwhelming majority of these will never get the chance of existing; but like anything else that exists in the world, there *must* be some that do. I can

---

[27] This is from a deterministic perspective. Also, if you believe that our existence is planned by a creator (who maybe will receive us in our afterlife) then you could accept that 'this is the way reality is'.

[28] Notice that we are talking about *sequences*, not *proportions*, of heads and tails. One-hundred percent heads is much less likely than, say, 50 heads and 50 tails because there is only one sequence that will give you the former, but a great many that will give you the latter.

only be astonished that Host [Me] exists if Host [Me] does exist! It is when I think of Soul [Me], my seemingly unique 'awareness of being', that I cannot escape being utterly astonished. Yet, if my Soul is integral to the person I am, and Host [Me] had never been born, then I would indeed never experience awareness of being. I wonder if you feel the same. Remember, it is the question whether, had any of the myriad conditions necessary for you to have been born not been in place, would you still experience being someone (same Soul, different Host) or would you have lost that chance? Being reincarnated at the end of each life would allow an affirmative response to the former possibility but, as we have seen, it is a highly problematic conjecture. Is there any other answer? Let's see.

PART III

PERSONAL IDENTITY

CHAPTER 8

A DILEMMA

So far, it seems that we have yet to discover any reason to contradict the assertion that each and every Soul is unique to the Person and Host associated with it. Before Host [You] existed—before you were born—there was no Soul [You]. When Host [You] stops 'doing' Person [You]—i.e. dies— Person [You] and Soul [You] cease to exist. For you and everyone else, before birth and after death there is only oblivion, no awareness of being.

Yet when we ask the question 'Why was I born the person I am?' matters become more problematic. One reply is to say that we are the person we are, and no explanation for this is required; asking 'Why was I born the person I am and not somebody else?' is meaningless, since there would be absolutely no way of knowing, and absolutely no detectable difference if, say, you were born as your next-door neighbour and your next-door neighbour were born as you (recall the meditation presented in chapter 3 when you imagined exchanging identities with a friend). The problem is that it leaves us with no satisfactory answers to those questions that follow on from this, notably whether, were any one of the myriad events and circumstances required for you to be born not to be in place, you would have lost the chance of experiencing 'awareness of being' any person or living creature at all.

The clue to how we might proceed lies in something that we, or at least I, have overlooked and that arises from how I defined 'Person' and our discussion of 'our being is in our doing' in chapter 6. It concerns the matter of our personal identity and whether this is preserved over time. What does it mean to say, 'I am the same person today that I was yesterday, last year, on my second birthday, and so on, and I shall be that same person tomorrow, next week, next year, in ten years' time, and so on'? We could also ask the same questions about another person—'Is *she* the same person today as she was yesterday?', etc. Remember that it is important to keep the discussion relevant to the question of 'sameness' in the sense of 'preservation of identity over time', specifically one's personal identity.

I think we will all agree that we all change in many ways over time—physically of course, but also with respect to our capabilities, memories, personality, attitudes, and so on. But we would still agree that we are 'the same person' throughout the whole of our lives in the sense of having the same identity, the person we are 'aware of being'. The person you were at any time in the past is not a different person to the one you are now in the same sense that the individual nearest to you at this moment is a different person to you; we can also say the same about the person you will be at any time in the future. At least we can say this of our subjective representation of the world. But does is hold for the world in reality?

Recall that in chapter 6 I asked you to consider whether a wave of your hand was the same wave on two separate occasions and I argued that it made no sense to ask this question, since a wave is not a thing but an activity, something your hand *does*. Hence we can't say it is the same wave or a different wave; the best we can do is to say whether your hand was waving in a similar or a different manner on the two occasions. I then applied the same reasoning to other things your body does (kick, punch, nod and so on) and to any activity of your brain, such as having a memory (remembering), a thought (thinking), a percept (perceiving) and a dream (dreaming). I concluded that Person [You] is not what you *are* but what Host [You] *does*.

Can you see what the implication of this is for the question of whether you are the same person over time? It must follow from the above discussion that just as with any of the activities listed, it is meaningless to say that Person [You] at one moment is the same as Person [You] at another!

Moreover, as Host [You] is constantly changing over time, both in its material composition and the way it is structured and functions, so the activity Person [You] must also become less similar—which, of course, it does.

So, according to our normal way of representing the world, when we ask whether our personal identity is preserved over time, the answer seems to be unequivocally yes; but adopt the above, more realistic perspective on the nature of Person, namely what the Host *does*, and it seems that the answer is no, or perhaps (and I think this is more correct) you could say the question does not make sense.

Am I missing something here? What about the Soul? In chapter 3 I equated the Soul with what I had already described in chapter 2 as one's 'awareness of being'. I added:

It also includes, under normal circumstances, awareness of the experience of always having been you in your past, and awareness of the anticipation of always being that person in the future. It is the 'I' in the questions 'Why am I the person I am?' and 'Why was I born this person and not someone else?'

In other words, the Soul is the means whereby we are aware that we are the same person from moment to moment and over longer periods of time, however much we change in our physical and psychological make-up and functioning.

However, in chapter 6 I said of the Soul:

It is an activity of the brain; or, just as in the case of the Person, we can say the Soul is an activity of the Host, something the Host does.

In other words, there is no such *thing* or *entity* as the Soul. Do we have to conclude from this that there is therefore no preservation of Soul over time? And if so, where does this leave us in our search for answers?

The next stage of our journey will be to explore in greater depth this dilemma and how it may be resolved. It is important first to provide much firmer support for the conclusions I have drawn in this chapter. There is in fact another, more well-trodden route that brings us to our current position, and this involves some celebrated philosophical paradoxes and conundrums.

CHAPTER 9

EXPLORING THE MEANING OF IDENTITY

I open this chapter by inviting you to consider a very well-known conundrum that has been discussed by many wise people for centuries, one with which you may well be familiar. This version is a modern one; shortly I shall refer to a similar but ancient and better-known version.

Is Leroy's car still 'Lucy'?
Allow me to introduce you to Leroy, who I would guess is now in his late fifties. For many years now, Leroy's pride and joy has been his Triumph sports car, which he named 'Lucy' when he first acquired it brand new. Today it is in the same pristine condition as when he bought it many years ago. But over the years, not only because of normal wear and tear, but also as a result of some rather serious mishaps, he has had to keep replacing old parts with brand new ones, though making sure that every replacement is of identical design to its original. In fact, today not one part of the vehicle belonged to the original car that Leroy bought. But it is still the same model, identical in structure, and it performs in exactly the

same way as the original when he bought it. And Leroy still calls it 'Lucy'. The question is 'Is Leroy's car still Lucy?'

Please allow yourself all the time you like to think about this before considering the next puzzles.

Variations on the paradox of Lucy

There are many versions of this paradox, and you might enjoy creating your own. The original version runs as follows.

The ship of Theseus refers to a vessel owned by the ancient mythical Greek king of that name. Over the course of many years after his death, it has been continually maintained by his followers by replacing damaged and worn-out parts with exact replicas. All the original parts have now been replaced. Is this still the ship of Theseus?

These kinds of questions are related to the idea of the preservation of identity over time. What decides that an object at a certain time is the same object at another time? (Please keep in mind that while the object may have changed over time, and in that sense is not 'the same', we are using 'same' here to mean 'its *identity* has not changed'. So I may say, for example, 'London now isn't the same London that I remember in my youth' but I'm still talking about the same city, London.) Now consider the following.

Imagine standing on the seashore and watching a big wave coming in. You take a photograph of it at twenty metres distance and again at ten metres distance. Have you photographed the same wave? We would all agree you have indeed done so. But a wave is a rhythmical up-and-down movement of water. It is this up-and-down *motion* that constitutes the wave, not water itself moving towards the shore. And this movement constantly alters in form and extent as it makes its way there. So, what is 'the same' about the wave that you photographed first and the wave that you photographed next? Clearly they are not the same thing if by *thing* we mean a material object or a collection of objects.

Now imagine that you are standing in one place looking at a river. Is the river you are looking at the same river that you were looking at a minute ago? Obviously none of the water will be the same after a minute has passed (recall the saying 'No person steps in the same river twice.') We can also ask, 'Is the river the same river at two different places?' For example, is the river Danube at its source in the Black Forest in Germany the same river that runs through Vienna, and is this the same river that runs through Bratislava, or Budapest, or Belgrade, and so on, until it empties into the Black Sea? Who or what decides the answers to all these questions?

Two variations on the theme of 'Is Leroy's car still Lucy?'

Returning to Leroy and Lucy, suppose that soon after Leroy bought his car and named it Lucy it was utterly destroyed in a fire. Not to be outdone, Leroy buys another brand new car, the same model as before, and again names it Lucy. Is this Lucy the same as the first Lucy? The two cars will certainly be identical in structure (and we'll assume colour) but I think we would all agree that they are two different cars; that is they have separate identities. Surely Leroy will accept this too; he will mourn the demise of the first Lucy, which had a short life and no longer exists, and hope, with the rest of us, that the second Lucy will be more fortunate.

We must now enquire what the difference is between this scenario and the first one, in which Leroy *over time* replaces all the parts of Lucy with new parts, so that the car remains identical to when he first bought it. Clearly there is no real difference; it seems that if we agree to accept that in the present variation of the puzzle, original Lucy is replaced by a different Lucy, then we must accept this to be the case in the first version. In the first version, the replacement has just taken longer and Leroy is wrong in thinking that Lucy's identity has been preserved over all that time.

Very well—but can you spot the snag? Don't worry if you can't, as I'll return to this in due course. Before I do, let's consider another variation of the Lucy puzzle. Suppose that over the years, Leroy does not faithfully replace each part of his car with an identical new part; rather, he chooses parts that are more up-to-date and thus different from the old parts. Suppose in time we have a car that is *structurally* very different from the original one, no part of which now remains. And suppose—as will certainly be the case—the new car performs in a very different way from the original one. Again we ask, 'Is it still Lucy?' Is its *identity* preserved? I think that in this case we would agree (and Leroy probably would too) that its identity has definitely not been preserved.

There are countless examples of this version of the puzzle. For instance, Nancy has just visited her old school, Newton Primary. The pupils have all changed, as have the teachers, and three years ago the entire building was demolished and the school was rebuilt on a different site. Is it still Nancy's old school, Newton Primary? You ask a similar question about the football club Nancy has supported all her life, the newspaper she has always read, and so on.

As you see, we can create lots of scenarios on the theme of preservation of identity and perform various thought experiments that raise many questions. Philosophers have done this over the centuries and have come up with various answers. I am going to suggest the answer I believe to be the most appropriate. Again keep in mind that we are aiming to arrive at a satisfactory answer to the question 'Am I the same person over time?'

First let us remind ourselves of the distinction 'the real world' and 'the subjective world' outlined in chapter 1 and Appendix I. In chapter 1 I invited you to think of two people, Ivan and Sonia, agreeing that they are both looking at some 'entity', in their case a car. I suggested that support for the assertion that the same entity exists for both of them in the real world comes when observations that they independently make about this entity concur—its agreed name (i.e. 'a car'), its colour and shape, its exact height, width and weight, and so on. Recall that I argued, 'This consistency compels us to believe that the entity in question has an independent existence in "the real world" separate from Sonia and Ivan; it is not something that only exists in each of their minds.'

Let's now suppose that the entity that Ivan and Sonia are experiencing is Lucy, Leroy's car. We explain to them that Leroy has faithfully restored his car over the years and now no part of it was on the original car when he obtained it. We then ask each of them 'Is this car still Lucy, the car that Leroy started off with all those years ago'?

Suppose that Ivan replies, 'Yes' and Sonia replies, 'No.' Clearly they are relying on different criteria to determine what constitutes 'being the same car'. These criteria may be explicit (that is, Ivan and Sonia can both explain what criteria they are using) but they may be implicitly understood by each of them. Whatever the case we next ask, 'Who is correct?' and this raises the question 'How do we find this out?' Is there an experiment we can perform that will unequivocally reveal who is right? The answer is no. The criteria that anyone uses to arrive at his or her answer exist not in 'the world out there' but in the world they each construct for themselves. Had the disagreement between Ivan and Sonia concerned, say, the question whether or not Leroy had indeed replaced every component of the original Lucy then we could settle the matter one way or the other in 'the world out there' by inspecting every part of the car. But we can do no such thing to resolve their present disagreement.

So the criteria that Leroy and Ivan adopt that define the car now as being Lucy, the car that Leroy originally acquired, are no less valid than those criteria adopted by Sonia, that define the car as no longer being Lucy. We can say the same for all the other examples given earlier.

However: the time has now come for us to return to 'the snag' that I mentioned earlier and that those who, like Sonia, say Leroy's car is no longer Lucy must confront. *At what point in the replacement process is Lucy no longer Lucy?* Suppose the first part that Leroy replaces is Lucy's interior rear-view mirror. Has his car now ceased to be Lucy? I think if you or I replaced the rear-view mirror in *our* car we would not immediately think that we now have a different car! Suppose that Leroy next replaces the offside wing mirror. Has his car now ceased to be Lucy? Suppose that he next replaces all the wheel trims. OK, I'll stop! I think by now you will have got my drift.

Interestingly, whether or not you side with Leroy and Ivan and consider Lucy's identity to be preserved, a similarly conundrum to the above arises with the scenario in which, over time, Leroy replaces every part with a more up-to-date one, eventually having a car that is structurally and functionally very different from the original Lucy. At what point in *this* process do we say the car is no longer Lucy?

Philosophers love these kinds of puzzles. Here's a couple more. A man who starts off with a full head of hair loses one hair at a time. At what point does he go from being a man who isn't bald to one who is? There's a similar one called the Heap Paradox (no, it's not named after me) about a heap of sand. There are no fixed answers to these questions except by agreement on some definition of what constitutes baldness, a heap, etc. and that agreement belongs in the subjective world, not in the real world independent of any sentient beings.

Let's summarise where we are before we get too carried away. It seems that what determines that an object at time 1 is the same object at time 2, in the sense that its identity is preserved over that time period, is that it is recognised as such by whoever is observing or thinking about it. People may disagree, but there is no objective way of proving who is correct. No one is right or wrong, because we are asking a question that is relevant to our subjective world and not to the world in reality; thus the answer depends on rules, criteria, meanings and so on that we ourselves create, that best suit our needs, and that are within the constraints of our own mental apparatus.[29]

The next step

Having considered the question of preservation of identity of inanimate objects that change over time we are now ready to think about the question of the preservation of our own personal identity. As we do this, keep in mind the foregoing discussion and the issues that have been raised. Does the above conclusion also apply? Let us see.

---

[29] During this discussion, you may have been wondering about solid, seemingly unchanging, objects. Surely a solid object like my desk is, if unaltered, the same object at different points in time? It isn't necessary to think about this now, but this question will crop up again later.

CHAPTER 10

WHAT DEFINES OUR PERSONAL IDENTITY?

In our chemistry lessons at school we learnt that everything that exists in the material world is made up of a finite number of elements—hydrogen, oxygen, copper, iron, etc. Elements may exist on their own in the form of atoms, or they may bond with each other to form many different compounds. For example atoms of the elements sodium and chlorine combine to form molecules of the compound sodium chloride (common salt), and hydrogen and oxygen atoms combine to form molecules of the compound water.

An individual person—a Host—is composed of trillions and trillions of molecules of compounds of a finite number of elements, namely carbon, oxygen, hydrogen, nitrogen, calcium and phosphorous, as well as (though in smaller quantities) several others. Some of these compounds are very simple, a good example being water, which accounts for around 50 to 60 per cent of body weight in adults (and higher than this for the brain and nervous system). Some compounds, such as proteins, consist of much larger and more complex molecules.

The molecules that make up the body are constantly being replaced; old molecules are expelled by the body and new ones are ingested. The rate that this occurs varies depending on the type of tissue but, at least theoretically, it could mean that over time there is a complete or near-complete turnover of body material at a molecular level.[30]

Does this allow us to say, 'There is hardly a molecule of me now that was present in my body X years ago and if so what is X?' This is the subject of some controversy but there does appear to be a valid case for making this kind of assertion, the number of years cited most often being somewhere between seven and ten. This uncertainty is not so important here, so let's just continue the discussion using the term 'X years'.[31]

So we can say that the physical material that comprised Host [You X years ago] has been (almost) completely replaced by the material that comprises Host [You now], but you are still the same individual—your personal identity has been retained.[32] Isn't this exactly what Leroy is insisting about his car Lucy?

Well, not quite. After X years, the 'newly constructed' Host [You now] is not an exact replica of Host [You X years ago] because the structure of Host [You] is constantly

---

[30] There may be no replacement for certain materials; 'non-living' tooth enamel is often cited in this regard.

[31] This issue is made more complicated by the fact that it is often discussed with respect to turnover of *cells* rather than molecules or atoms. For present purposes I consider it better to talk about replacement at the molecular level. Also, the objection has been raised that since all atoms of the same element are absolutely identical, it is meaningless to talk about one atom or molecule replacing another, as there would be no way of detecting that this had happened. I am doubtful about the utility of such arguments in the present context.

[32] You may appreciate here the cogency of thinking of Person [You] not as an object but as an activity of Host [You].

changing, owing to maturation and aging, experience, illness, injury, and so on. This is analogous to the version of the paradox in which Leroy replaces each new part of Lucy with one that is slightly different so that the car gradually becomes structurally and functionally less like Lucy at the time Leroy acquired her.

I have suggested that whether we say the two cars are the same is effectively a matter of social convention and is not one that arises in the real world. The question now is 'Does this also apply to human beings?'

Meditation

With the forgoing in mind, I invite you to consider the following scenario. It is, let's say, a summer's day sometime in the 1940s. We are in the countryside and are watching two five-year-old girls, Anne and Mary, happily playing together by a river. I now ask you, 'Are Anne and Mary the same person or two different people?' There can only be one answer, yes or no, with no 'in-betweens', 'ifs' or 'buts'. Obviously your answer is that they *are* two different people!

Now we move forward in time, and we are paying a visit to an old persons' care home where, among the residents, we see a frail old lady who is confined to a wheelchair. This is Anne, eighty years later.

I now ask you, 'Is the Anne whom we saw playing with Mary all those years ago the same Anne whom we now see years later in the care home? Or are they two different people?' Again there can only be one answer, yes or no, with no 'in-betweens', 'ifs' or 'buts'. This time, your reply is that they are the same person. For good measure, you would also say categorically that old Anne is not the same person as young Mary. And I would have to agree with you! Thus we have no doubt that Anne's identity has been preserved over all these years.

But why do we say this? In their physical make-up— materially and structurally—old and young Anne are completely different. In this respect also, old Anne and young Anne may be more different than are young Anne and young Mary. And as regards what they actually do (remember, 'our being is in our doing'), young Anne and young Mary again appear to have much more in common than young Anne and old Anne.

One answer could be that old Anne has virtually the same DNA as young Anne. But even without DNA evidence, we would have no hesitation in declaring that old and young Anne are one and the same person. And what if Anne and Mary are identical twins, and therefore have the same DNA? Wouldn't we still consider them to be different persons?

This meditation is about the following question. What is it that makes us insist that old Anne and young Anne are the same person? I invite you to pause for a while and think about this.

---0---

Further deliberations
Let us continue thinking about the above meditation. In our everyday perception of the world we are unequivocal in saying that old Anne and young Anne are the same person. Yet physically, they are very different. Not only do they have relatively few molecules in common, Host [Young Anne] and Host [Old Anne] are structurally very different. (We need to remember that we are speaking mainly about the nervous systems—especially the brains—of young and old Anne. Particularly at the microscopic level, and especially at the inter-neuronal connections, they will be very different.) And because they are structurally so different, Host [Young Anne] and Host [Old Anne] engage in very different activities as Person [Young Anne] and Person [Old Anne] with respect to their thoughts, explicit and implicit memories, intellectual skills, and even their personalities. Yet, we still have no hesitation in saying that Old Anne is *the same person* as young

Anne. Why? (You may find the question 'Is a river the same river at two different places, e.g. at its source and at its estuary?' an apposite analogy here.)

There are at least two responses to this question that we may consider here. The first is to recall the 'snag' that I introduced in the previous chapter when discussing the paradox of Leroy's car Lucy. In the case of Anne we say, 'If old Anne is not the same person as young Anne, there must have been a point in Anne's life when this change of personal identity occurred.' I think we would become stuck in any search for an objective way of identifying when this moment occurred.

A second response to the question runs as follows. Think of Anne and Mary playing together as children. Suppose something terrible befalls young Anne while she is playing, say she falls in the river and drowns. Then there would be no future Anne doing all the activities and having all the experiences in her life that she would otherwise do and have. There would be no Host [Old Anne] and no Person [Old Anne]. So that seems to settle it. Destroy Host [Young Anne], and hence Person [Young Anne], and you also eliminate Person [Old Anne]. From this and the first response, it may be argued that young and old Anne are indeed the same person.

This argument may seem very compelling, and it *is* compelling if we have in mind what we normally mean by 'the same person'. If, for example, someone tried to tell us that the person sitting in the care home is Anne, the girl who used to play with Mary when she was five, and we knew for a fact that Anne had died some years ago, we would state adamantly, 'No, that can't be Anne, it must be someone else!' But it doesn't help us with the question whether preservation of identity over time is something that exists *in reality* and not just in the way we think of the world. Consider what happens when we apply this argument to the question of preservation of identity of those inanimate objects that we discussed earlier. The equivalent argument in, say, the case of Leroy's car Lucy would be as follows: the present Lucy must have the same identity as the original Lucy since it would not exist now if at some point Lucy had been destroyed.

In the next chapter we shall consider some thought experiments that address this matter more directly. If at present you are not entirely convinced about the way this discussion is proceeding, it may be because you have noticed that I am overlooking one important difference between humans and cars. Human beings are conscious and self-aware. Moreover, however much Host [Anne], and hence Person [Anne], changes, Host [Anne] will always be uniquely able to recall events and happenings in Anne's life at almost any age 'as Anne experienced them'. It will 'know' Anne in a way that no other Host or Person is capable of. Anne in her eighties, still possessed of her mental faculties, would not hesitate to tell us that she is indeed 'the same person' as young Anne or, for that matter, Anne at any time in her life up to the present. Her Soul has not changed in the sense that she has had no awareness of being anybody except this person Anne. Soul [Anne], it seems, confirms the preservation of Person [Anne] over time, despite the transformation of Host [Anne].

How would the fact that old Anne has dementia and has lost all her memories, even her knowledge of who she is, affect these arguments? Surely in these circumstances, Soul [Old Anne] can't confirm the preservation of her personal identity over time.

One reply to this is as follows. I have no doubt that there are many experiences in your life of which you have no recollection—i.e. Host [You] is unable to engage in the activity of remembering those events. I myself have a photograph of our neighbourhood pageant celebrating Queen Elizabeth II's Coronation in 1953. There I am, in the role of the infant Prince Charles, complete with chubby cheeks and big ears. I have absolutely no memory of this occasion, but I have no problem accepting that the person in the photograph is the same person who is now looking at the photograph. And I would not dispute that the 'I' who was aware of engaging in the above activity at the time is the same 'I' who is now aware of looking at the photograph of this activity decades later. In other words, Soul [Me] is the same.

As I say, you will have many such examples of your own; indeed reliable long-term memories are very unlikely for events that occurred before the age of around 2½ years. Nor do they have to be events from long ago; I am often amazed, and not a little disconcerted, when I discover that I have no recollection of some not insignificant event—e.g. eating in a particular restaurant—that I experienced only a few months previously. But should my wife, who was there at the time, recall the event, I would not immediately insist to her that she must have been with someone else. Nor would I consider that it must have been a different 'I' that was aware of being Person [Me] in the restaurant! In a manner of speaking, we assume that this 'constancy of the Soul' applies whether or not we can now recall the incidents in question.

We can adopt a similar stance when thinking of experiences *that have yet to happen,* and indeed I find this more convincing than considering past events when arguing for the constancy of the Soul. Think of Anne at the age of sixty. She is very much alert and in full possession of her mental faculties. Sadly she is informed by her doctor that although she is fine now, she has a medical condition that is incurable and which will inevitably destroy her brain cells, causing her gradually to lose all her mental abilities, including her short- and long-term memory. Naturally Anne is horrified by this news. She thinks, 'This is *my* fate. This is going to happen to *me.*' That is, the 'I' that is aware of being the Anne who is experiencing and reacting to this shocking news is the same 'I' that will be aware of being the Anne who is experiencing profound dementia, even though by then she will have lost all her memories. And surely she is right. Suppose, for example, that when she reaches the age of sixty-five and starts to be aware of symptoms of her illness, she recalls the occasion when her doctor broke the bad news to her and she said to herself, 'This is *my* fate.' And surely it should make no difference if, by then, her illness has progressed to the point where she has no memory of that event.

So can we say that the thing that is constant and that decides that each one of us is the same person over time, is what we have defined as our Soul, our 'awareness of being'?

Or could it be that we have overlooked something that changes all of this? Let us see.

Afterthoughts

In the discussion of preservation of personal identity concerning the case of Anne in her eighties, some of our arguments were based on her aging or having dementia as being gradual processes of change. For example, I pointed to the 'snag' in arguing that old Anne is no longer the same person as young Anne, namely that we would have to identify a point (or points) in time when Anne's identity changes. But suppose that in the case of Anne with dementia, the damage to her brain resulted from a sudden head injury. Could we not say that the above 'snag' does not apply and that at the moment the injury occurred, Anne ceased to be the person she had been up until then?

My answer to this is that it shouldn't make any difference to the question of the preservation of Anne's personal identity how she acquired the damage to her brain, whether suddenly or gradually over a period of time. As it happens, I once saw someone professionally who, for no apparent reason, suddenly had no memory of who she was, where she lived, and what she had done in life up until then. There was no question but that she was the same person as before this event, and indeed her immediate actions were to set about answering the question 'Who am I?' and finding her way home. Her longer-term aim was to do her best to resume the life she had before.

Relatedly, consider this rather unpleasant scenario. Someone you love is murdered. Immediately following the act, the perpetrator receives a head injury causing him to have no memory of his life up until then, including his identity. The police decide not to prosecute, as he is no longer the person who committed the offence. Would you be angry? I bet you would! And so would I.

CHAPTER 11

'WHO AM I?'

Is my personal identity preserved over time? Despite the molecular constituents of my entire body (Host [Me]) being continuously added to, replaced or discarded, am I the same person now as I was in the past and will be in the future? In the last chapter we examined some arguments for answering yes and some objections to these. Seemingly, one of the most compelling arguments in favour was based on what I have defined throughout our journey so far as the Soul, our awareness of being. Soul [Me] appears to be constant throughout my life in the sense that I am uniquely able to remember experiences in my earlier life as they happened *to me*, to experience events in my present life as happening to *the same me*, and to anticipate future experiences and later to live through them as *the same me*, even recalling my earlier anticipation of them. That I often cannot remember such events hardly justifies the assertion that in such cases continuity of personal identity has not been maintained.

Let us now consider two well-known thought experiments that challenge this way of thinking and indeed call into question the whole idea that our personal identity is preserved over time.

A meditation on 'Who am I'

Imagine that in the future, scientists will have developed a method of 'teleportation' whereby objects, including human beings, may be transported from one place to another at the speed of light, as in the *Star Trek* TV series, when Captain Kirk gives the order 'Beam me up, Scotty!', though I believe he never used these precise words).

Imagine that the system is regularly used to transport workers who are commuting from the Earth to the Moon and back, just as people nowadays commute, say, from Oxford to London and back on high-speed trains. Imagine you are one such commuter.

What happens is that you enter a scanner on the Earth (perhaps something like an MRI scanner), the operator presses a button, and the scanner plots the exact co-ordinates of every atom in your body.[33] This information is encoded on a computer and is transmitted at or close to the speed of light to a sophisticated machine on the Moon, where the information is immediately decoded. You are then reconstructed atom-for-atom from local materials. Once you are fully replicated, you are ready to continue your journey to work by more conventional means. Also, exactly at the point of transmission of the scanned information to the Moon, your body on the Earth is instantaneously destroyed. All of this applies on the return journey, from the Moon to the base on Earth.

Suppose you are a scientist in this futuristic scenario. You live with your spouse or partner on planet Earth but you have just been offered an exciting job that means you will have to

---

[33] You may immediately want to point out the insuperable problem of locating the exact positions of atoms, but let's suppose that this problem has been overcome—it's only a thought experiment!

commute by teleportation to the Moon and back every working day. How do you feel about that? Imagine getting ready to step into the teleporter for the first time. Would you happily go ahead or would you have second thoughts? For the purposes of this exercise let's assume that you are reassured that the procedure is guaranteed to go ahead as planned—there's no possibility of any breakdown in the system. So just pause for a few moments now and think about the question posed.

If your answer is that you are perfectly happy to go ahead with the teleportation process on this and every other occasion, then why? Something must reassure you that when you step out of the teleporter at your destination—in the case of your very first journey, the Moon—you are the same person that stepped into the teleporter at the start of your journey on Earth. In other words, your personal identity has been preserved. This reassurance may be derived from the following argument, using the terminology of this book. Although Host [You] is destroyed by the teleportation process, an identical copy is constructed. And since Person [You] is defined as what Host [You] does, it follows that Person [You] is preserved. So we have good reason to believe that, having undergone teleportation, you will walk away with the feeling that you are the same person as when you started out, just as when you make any journey by more conventional means (and, apparently, just like the crew of the starship *Enterprise*). Nothing about you will have changed and continuity of personal identity will be maintained. Recall also that the hypothetical teleportation experiment is happening naturally to you and everyone else, though at a much slower rate, as the atoms of your body are continuously being replaced and your body reconstructed.

If, on the other hand, you still don't feel happy with the idea of being teleported, then why? The most likely answer is that you cannot escape the thought that at the outset of your journey, you—the person you are at that point in your life—

are destroyed. You are killed—murdered even! It doesn't matter that another copy of you, however exact, will be created; nor does it matter that this copy of you will have the same sense of self as you. As far as you're concerned it's still only a copy: your personal identity has most definitely not been preserved!

If you are correct, then in what sense will you be killed? What does it mean to say that when you enter the teleporter you are about to die? After all, as we have argued above, the 'you' that exits the teleporter at your destination will certainly *feel* that they are the same person as the one who entered the teleporter at the outset, just as if, say, the journey were made in a spacecraft and you'd been asleep the whole way; it will seem to *that* 'you' that life has continued as normal.

Speaking for myself, if I imagine that at the start of teleportation I am thinking that I am about to die, it will be because I believe that my 'awareness of being' is about to cease. The person who emerges from the teleporter station at the destination may, in every sense detectable by him or her and everyone else, be the person I am aware of being right now. However it won't be 'I' who will be aware of being that person, it will be some other 'I'; the former 'I' will no longer exist. That is, the fate of 'I' prior to teleportation is oblivion, just as when we die in any other context.

What I am now saying, in the terminology of this book, is that the thing that will change as a result of my teleportation is Soul [Me]. Remember, Soul [Me] is my awareness of being the person I am, have been, and will be in the future. Even though I might accept the argument that Person [Me]—what Host [Me] does—will be preserved, Soul [Me] will no longer exist; in a manner of speaking the person I am after teleportation 'has a different Soul'. In this sense my personal identity will have changed.

To reiterate, the paradox of this way of thinking is that none of it will be apparent to the copy of me or to anyone else. It is rather reminiscent of the meditation in chapter 3 when I asked you to imagine yourself becoming your friend and *vice versa*—i.e. swapping Souls. And if you did pluck up courage and undergo teleportation, when it's over you would probably think to yourself, with some relief, something like, 'Oh I was wrong; I'm still me!' That is, you will experience continuity of personal identity.

Which of the above arguments is the correct one? Indeed, *is* there a correct way of looking at this scenario? Where do you, the reader, stand on this issue? I invite you to think what your point of view is before considering a variation of the teleportation thought experiment.

Another meditation on 'Who am I?'

Suppose in the above scenario you accepted the offer of the job on the Moon and have been doing it for a year now. Imagine that one morning you set out from home to the teleportation station, thinking as usual about what you want to achieve on the Moon that day. Once at the station you are enclosed in the scanner. The transmission of your atomic coordinates to the Moon and your reconstitution there will take time, but apart from the change of scenery once you've arrived, there will be no discontinuity apparent to you.

Once reconstituted on the Moon, you then make the journey to your workplace. Your day passes and the time comes for you to return to the Moon station for your transmission back to Earth. You enter the scanner and wait for the operator to press the button that starts the whole process. As usual, you think about what you have achieved that day. Let's suppose things didn't quite go as planned: you had an argument with a colleague who was being very unhelpful, and you now recall with some surprise the anger that you experienced with this person at the time. However, you also remind yourself that that evening, back on Earth, some old school friends are coming round for a barbecue and you console yourself with the pleasurable anticipation of seeing them again.

Then the operator presses the button and, in what seems like a brief moment, you are back at the station on Earth. As on many previous occasions, you go through all the medical and security checks, sign out and continue your journey by more conventional means. Again you think back to the argument with your colleague and then tell yourself to forget it and think about seeing your friends.

Well, apart from the extremely unusual background to this thought experiment, there does not appear to be any reason for you to have any qualms about the teleportation process. You are familiar with the two arguments that I have outlined above, and your viewpoint, based on your one-year's experience of being a teleportee, is that, as with any other method of commuting, your personal identity has been preserved throughout; after all, if you had been repeatedly killed, surely you would be the one to know about it! On each occasion, all parts of Host [You] have been completely reconstituted, but this process happens naturally anyway—albeit gradually, over a span of several years. In fact, as with Lucy in the original version of the thought experiment, you have been reconstituted in exactly the same form, so we do not even have to worry about any change of structure and function. Nothing has ever appeared to be amiss.

Except that on this occasion, something *is* amiss. While you are checking out of the station back on Earth, unbeknown to you, 'you' on the Moon (Host [You prior to teleportation]) are being withdrawn from the scanner and, expecting to find yourself on Earth, to your surprise you are still at the Moon station. The rather flustered operator then explains that there has been a slight technical glitch that will only take a moment to fix, and then you'll be back in the teleporter. When you ask her what has happened, she explains that the scanning, encoding, and transmission phases have gone exactly to plan, but the destruction phase has yet to be enacted. 'But don't worry—it'll only take a minute to put right,' she says. You patiently wait for the fault to be corrected. You continue with your musings, impatient to get back to Earth and prepare for the barbecue.

I now invite you to meditate on the paradoxes and consequences of the above scenario. Do you, the person who is still on the Moon, want the destruction stage to be carried out now? If so, what happens to you? Once the technical glitch has been rectified and the process continues, will there be any real difference between what has happened on *this* occasion and what has happened on all previous occasions?

CHAPTER 12

IMPASSE

At the end of the last chapter I left you waiting on the Moon, as you have often done in this futuristic scenario, for the teleportation process to be completed. Are you keen for the operator to complete the process—the usual, though in this case slightly delayed, destruction of your body?

What follows now is consistent with what most people with whom I have discussed this scenario have told me is their response, and it is mine also. If yours is different it does not mean that you are wrong; I do not believe that there is necessarily a right and a wrong answer, rather there are different points of view.

If your reaction is similar to mine, you will suddenly have the chilling realisation that the reconstructed you is already at the Earth station waiting for the medical and security checks before setting off home to prepare for the barbecue. For you on the Moon, destruction means just that—oblivion. Surely you are going to plead with the operator to halt the proceedings!

Let's study this more closely. While waiting on the Moon you have been eagerly anticipating the barbecue with your friends back on Earth that evening. You have thus assumed implicitly that the 'you' that is aware of waiting to be teleported back to Earth is the same 'you' that will be aware of experiencing those pleasurable activities to come. This is no different from how you normally think about yourself; in our terminology, this is preservation of personal identity by continuity of Soul [You], as we have previously discussed. But now, having been informed of the glitch, you think, 'It won't be me here on the Moon who will be aware of enjoying those pleasures; it is the reconstructed me who is now already back on Earth. By the time the barbecue is happening I shall be dead!'

Of course the reconstructed you on Earth is oblivious to all of this. You on Earth believe that you are the same person who, back on the Moon, experienced the argument with your colleague, the eager anticipation of meeting your friends that evening, and so on. But if someone were to explain to you on Earth what was happening on the Moon at that moment, you would consider that it was not *you* who was aware of having those experiences at the time, or indeed anything else that you were involved with on the Moon that day. That 'you' is still on the Moon!

And there is more to come. As both versions of you are contemplating what's happened, another awful realisation comes to mind. *Even without the glitch*, all the above would still apply. In other words, on every previous occasion you have been teleported between the Earth and the Moon, your Soul has been terminated. Each time that, prior to teleportation, you have been thinking about the things you will experience following teleportation, it has not been 'you now' who is going to be aware of having those experiences; it will be, let us say, 'you next'; 'you now' (Soul [You now]) will have ceased to exist. And each time that, following teleportation, you have been thinking *back* on your experiences prior to teleportation, it has not been 'you now' who was aware of having those experiences as they happened, it has been 'you

then'; and 'you then' (Soul [You then]) has by that stage
ceased to exist.[34]

All of this appears to support the second of the two
arguments about teleportation that we discussed in the
previous chapter, namely that you, the teleportee, are killed
in the process, even if there are no glitches, and replaced by
a copy. So the next time you are ready to be teleported you
will immediately be faced with the question 'What happens
to me when I die, as I am surely going to now?' And the
rational answer is 'oblivion'—it's entirely irrelevant that an
exact living copy of you will be created in the process. If you
accept this, then you are most unlikely to step into the
teleporter again. Take up an Earth-bound job instead!

Implications
Have we arrived at the definitive answer? I'm not sure. We
still have the paradox that whether the first or the second
argument applies (preservation of personal identity or its
obverse) makes absolutely no detectable difference to the
outcome; in either case, the teleported individual thinks, feels
and behaves in exactly the same way as they would do had
they simply made their journey by other means. Moreover,
we also have the consideration that the hypothetical
teleportation experiment is actually happening to all of us
naturally, although the deconstruction-reconstruction
process occurs in slow motion. Also, not only are the
molecules being replaced; structurally we change with the
aging process. Therefore, we change functionally: each Host
changes in respect of what it *does*—thinks differently,

---

[34] You may wonder whether the coexistence in time of the original
and reconstructed you in the 'technical glitch' scenario means that
the comparison with the usual scenario, in which there is no such
co-existence, is valid. Would there be any detectable differences,
physical or subjective, between the two reconstructed 'yous' in the
two scenarios? None at all.

remembers differently, feels differently, and so on.[35] Hence, when you think of yourself in, say, nine years' time, you are in the same hypothetical position as described earlier when you realise that for Soul [You prior to teleportation], teleportation means death and oblivion. If we take this as it stands, it seems to imply that Soul [You now], as we have conceived it, is not the same as Soul [You nine years ahead from now] or Soul [You nine years ago]. And there is more that follows from this: by this reasoning, Soul [You in one year's time] is not the same as Soul [You eight years ago]. In which case Soul [You now] can't be the same as *both* Soul [You in one year's time] *and* Soul [You eight years ago], and so on and on for any period of time. Recall also that there is another conundrum here. If Soul [You in nine years] is not the same as Soul [You now], at what moment in those nine years did the change occur?

In chapter 10 we concluded that what we have defined as our Soul is the one thing that is constant in our lives and defines our personal identity and its preservation over time. Just like Anne in the care home, we accept that those personal events in our past, even those we have now forgotten, were experienced by the same individual that we are now, however much we have changed, similarly those events that we anticipate occurring in our future. But it now appears that, compelling as this may seem, it is an illusion.

So where does this leave us in the search for answers to our questions? It now seems that asking 'Why was I born the person I am?', 'What happens to me when I die?', and so on is indeed based on faulty assumptions if, even within our own lifetime, preservation of our personal identity from moment

---

[35] It may be argued that teleportation and the natural transformation of a Host are different, since the latter takes place within one Host, as it were, whereas the former involves the creation of a separate Host. However, the net outcome is exactly the same in each case, except that the Host in the natural reconstruction process is always changing structurally.

to moment is illusory. Clearly, we need to pause and do some rethinking before deciding which direction we should now take in order to continue with our journey.

CHAPTER 13

A WAY FORWARD

It is not difficult to think of variations of the teleportation thought experiment that raise all sorts of questions and paradoxes and you might enjoy making up some of your own. I do not wish to burden you with too many of these, but there are two more that it might be worth your while looking at and I have put these in Appendix II. You may wish to look at them now or later or not at all. Their purpose is to reinforce the conclusions that I outlined in the previous chapter.

Where does this leave us?
If we continue with the metaphor that likens our search for answers to a journey, then we seem to have arrived at an impasse. In essence, our journey has been a search for the nature of the Soul—our awareness of being—and its fate when our physical form, and thus the person we are aware of being, ceases to exist. Does it continue in some form—for example awareness of being some other sentient being—or does it also cease to exist ('oblivion')? This has required us to examine what we mean by our 'personal identity' and its

preservation over time. We started off by acknowledging that what we have identified as Host and Person, i.e. what the Host *does*, change markedly over time, but our Soul—our awareness of being who we are—remains 'the same', thus preserving our sense of identity over time. This is consistent with our whole experience. However, our thought experiments have brought us to the stage where it seems we are forced to conclude that the idea that, even from moment to moment and over our own lifetime, our personal identity, and hence our Soul, is something that is 'the same', is an illusion after all.[36]

Where do we go now?

As with any journey, if we become lost or reach what appears to be a dead end, the usual thing to do is to retrace our steps and see where we might have taken a wrong turning. Maybe once again we have encountered the need to clearly distinguish our subjective and objective worlds and conclude that our overwhelming sense of preservation of personal identity belongs to the former, not the latter. Note that it is not quite appropriate to express this by saying that personal identity is *not* preserved over time; rather it is more accurate to say that **preservation of personal identity has no meaning in reality**—it is a concept that we can simply ignore.

Have we arrived at the point where we must also jettison the concepts of Host, Person and Soul as I have defined them for you? As I stated at the outset, this tripartite division is not intended as an *accurate* representation of reality; rather it is 'a working model' that can help us move forward in our quest and, like all working models, it has its limitations. Actually, I believe that it still has great utility at this stage of

---

[36] A more meticulous discussion of the question of the preservation of personal identity is provided by the British philosopher Derek Parfit (1984).

our journey. But we now find ourselves having to abandon the idea of 'preservation of identity' in relation to Host, Person, *and* Soul. So where do we go from here?[37]

The concept of 'discrete conscious event'

My response to this question is to introduce a concept that I shall call a 'discrete conscious event' (or 'experience'), one that occurs at 'a moment in time'. Examples are as follows: reading a particular word or phrase, hearing the telephone ring, noticing an itchy sensation somewhere on your skin, or recalling someone's name you have been trying to remember. There are of course an unimaginable number of such discrete conscious events (DCEs) throughout your lifetime, let alone the history of the universe. In the latter case they occur at minute places in the universe where matter is organised in such a way that it is capable of consciousness. I am suggesting that we treat each one as a separate event, the activity of one *unique* Host. The qualifier 'unique' is important here: every DCE that occurs in the universe is unique and must therefore be associated with a Host that is itself uniquely structured to engage in that activity[38]. A DCE also includes the Host's being aware of itself and its own activity;

---

[37] I have earlier referred to preservation of identity over time as an 'illusion' and other writers do likewise. I believe this term to be appropriate, but we must remember that illusions are not like hallucinations, i.e. inventions of the mind that are not present in reality. More correctly, illusions are interpretations of reality (e.g. optical illusions). So, consistent with this book's philosophy (if it's on the map it's part of the territory), our sense of preservation of identity is an *adaptive* response to circumstances and events in the real world. In due course we shall need to explore in greater depth how it comes about that our sense of personal identity is so compelling.

[38] In terms of what we have identified as, say, Host [You], with each successive DCE Host [You] is continuously changing in its composition and structure over the whole of your lifetime.

this is what I have equated with the concept 'having a Soul'. Also, a DCE is part of the broader activity that that Host engages in, namely 'being (i.e. doing) a Person'.

And so we are setting aside the idea of continuity of personal identity over time and considering that each and every conscious experience is associated with one unique Host. Thus we have no need to trouble ourselves unduly with the questions about preservation of self and identity in the various paradoxes and thought experiments we have already discussed. In this way, we shall find that our journey is made much easier.

It will be apparent to you that what is being proposed here is the very opposite of what we experience at any time, namely that what I have identified as a 'discrete conscious event' is always experienced as occurring within a continuous, ongoing stream of consciousness that belongs uniquely to the person one is. Now I am asking you to ignore this subjective impression and consider all such conscious experiences as separate events. You may find it very difficult to accept this second way of thinking, but please remember that it is one particular way of looking at the phenomena we are exploring. It is not a matter of whether it is 'the correct way', but very importantly, it is not an incorrect way; that is, it is not contradicted by our existing knowledge about the world. Neither are we making any *additional* assumptions; we are merely excluding from our deliberations this business of 'sameness'—continuity of personal identity—that we normally take for granted but which is the source of such confusion.

The space-time universe

A concept that may make things a little easier is that of space-time. Let us consider a well-documented historical event: the assassination of Thomas Becket who, on December 29, 1170, was murdered at the High Altar of Canterbury Cathedral by four knights, believing that they were carrying out the wishes of King Henry II. We cannot go back in time to witness the very moment when his assassins struck him down, but would you agree that we can visit the very spot where this happened?

Yes, if we mean the very spot in Canterbury Cathedral where he was murdered. But if we are talking about the exact place in the universe, then first of all, at the time of Becket's assassination the Earth was, as usual, spinning on its axis. It was also revolving around the Sun, and the Sun and its solar system were moving together through space. So by these facts alone, it is not possible for us to return to the very spot *in the universe* where the assassination took place. But according to our usual way of understanding time, that very location no longer exists anyway—neither did it exist *before* the assassination. This is because when this event happened (as with any event) the universe was expanding just as it had always been doing before and has continued to do ever since. It is not just that the galaxies are moving apart: space has been expanding relentlessly since the universe was created. We can therefore no more return to that *specific place* in the universe where the event occurred than we can return to the *moment in time* that it occurred.[39]

Nowadays scientists represent space and time as a unitary concept, 'space-time' and any event—anything that happens—may be uniquely located in space-time according to four dimensions, the three dimensions of space and the one of time[40]. And this includes the event we have called a

---

[39] Ancient philosophers were aware of this idea that the world is in a state of 'perpetual (or eternal) flux', which links to our discussions concerning preservation of identity.

[40] Some scientists now consider that both space and time are not 'fundamental properties' of the universe but 'emerge' from fundamental properties that existed at the time of, or even before, 'the Big Bang'. Here, it is simply considered that this four-dimensional representation is an advance on the usual way our minds conceive the structure of the universe.

DCE. So think, if you can, of a four-dimensional universe in which there are rare, but nevertheless countless locations in space-time at which a Host (unique to that location) is engaged in the activity of a DCE. One such event is a Host that is aware of being me—MH—sitting at his desk at 15:58 hours on September 15, 2021, hearing one of his cats coming through the cat-flap.

Before closing this chapter, as is so often the case in this book I should make clear that despite the conclusions we have reached it will still be far easier to communicate to you in the language of our subjective representation of the world, in this case based on the premise that you and I and everybody else retain our unique identity over time. When necessary, however, I shall explicitly refer to these radically different ways of representing reality.

A meditation on the meaning of 'now'

It is still important for us to consider in greater depth how our compelling sense of continuity of self or personal identity from moment to moment over our entire lifetime comes about if we are now considering our conscious experience to be, in a manner of speaking, a succession of DCEs each with its unique Host, and Person. However, it will be easier if we defer this until we have addressed a matter of great significance that is now looming large before us, namely the nature of time.

I stated earlier that any DCE occurs at 'a moment in time'. I admit that this expression is rather vague—I am not specifying how long this moment is. But it is a very special moment. It is what we experience as *now*. Thus we may also refer to a DCE as 'a now experience'.

Once again imagine the entire history of the universe— past, present *and* future—in four-dimensional space-time and all the DCEs that occur within it. Like any other activity, some are 'now experiences' that happened in the universe's past, some are 'now experiences' occurring in the universe's present, and some are 'now experiences' in the universe's future and have yet to occur. In other words, they no longer exist, they exist, or they have yet to exist. This is a static image, but time marches on relentlessly; those DCEs that exist in the present do so momentarily before joining those in the past, likewise those in the future when their turn arrives.

Though somewhat unusual, this image of the universe is still consistent with our everyday way of conceiving time and existence. But how accurately does it mirror reality? This represents our task for the next stage of our journey, when we shall once again find ourselves having to make some radical and surprising changes to how we normally think of our world.

All that is required for the moment is for me to invite you to meditate on this question: 'What exactly do *you* mean by the word "now"?'

PART IV

ABOUT TIME

CHAPTER 14

THE MEANING OF 'THE PRESENT'

The conclusions arrived at in the previous section are not the end point of how we are to represent a discrete conscious event: it is an interim step. So let us hold on to this concept while we explore a topic that is important for answering our questions on the fate of the Soul. This is the nature of time. Let us first briefly remind ourselves of some basic information about time.

Most scientists now consider that there is overwhelming evidence that, *expressed in simple terms*, our universe began around 13.8 billion years ago as an infinitesimally small 'point'. Since then ('the Big Bang') it has continued its expansion and of the different options, indefinite expansion seems to be the outcome scientists currently prefer. Let's make the—some would say—contentious assumption that time was created at the moment of 'the Big Bang'. Hence we can, at least in theory, identify any moment in our universe's history by reference to the number of units of time that have passed since its inception.

Our measurement of time is based on certain regular activities such as the movement of the hands of a clock, the orbit of the Earth around the Sun (one orbit equalling one year), the rotation of the Earth on its axis (one rotation equalling one day), and so on. Thus, although we tend to think of time as being measured by a kind of invisible scale, this scale is clearly not 'invisible': *it* also has to be part of the universe.

Using such measurements, we can give the timing of a particular event by reference to some other event that came before or is due to come after that event. For instance, we can say that our solar system began to form roughly 9 billion years after 'the Big Bang'; that the philosopher Socrates died 399 years before the notional birth of Jesus Christ; that the First World War ended 1,918 years after the aforementioned event; that Sue went off to university when she was 18 (i.e. 18 years after her birth); that I was wide awake this morning one hour before my alarm was due to go off; and so on.

Another property of time that seems indisputable to us is that, in a manner of speaking, it 'moves forward'. Thus, we may represent time as like a train moving along and carrying us with it. We meet future events on the way and thus they are in the present; when they are over we leave them behind 'in the past'. Alternatively, we may imagine that *we* are stationery and events are moving past us—future events are coming towards us, they pass us, and then they recede into the distance (the past) as other events approach and arrive.

Although time seems to pass by at varying 'speeds'— appearing to go very slowly when we are bored, or quickly when we are having a good time—all the information we have in our everyday life tells us that time always passes 'at the same rate'. If, say, you and a friend are in a situation where for one of you time is dragging but not for the other, when it is over and you both look at your watches they will still be in agreement; both of you would expect this to be the case, despite your differing subjective impressions. However, it is a fact that the passage of time is affected by physical factors such as gravity, acceleration, and the velocity of the timer relative to that of the event being timed. This was first theorised by Albert Einstein and because of advances in technology, notably the precision whereby time can be measured, has since been shown to be the case. For example, gravity is associated with the slowing down of time so that if you are on top of the Eiffel Tower, time will be going faster than if you are standing at the bottom, because the Earth's gravity is weaker at the top (and not because you are having a more interesting time there!) I should add that this effect is only measurable in billionths of a second. Here we have a good illustration of how science brings us closer to understanding the nature of the real world in a way that contradicts how we habitually represent it in our mind.

The above considerations need not concern us here, however. What is important now is to remind ourselves that, figuratively speaking, for us time moves smoothly and relentlessly in the same direction and there are strict laws for the ordering of events in time. For example, an event that causes another event to occur must always precede that event: I can make you laugh—or more likely groan—by telling you a joke, but the joke must come first. Also, we cannot travel backwards in time or, except by the natural 'flow' of time, forwards.

Time past, time present and time future
To reiterate, for us, events occur in a fixed order. For instance, we can say that in 1170, Thomas Becket was murdered in Canterbury Cathedral. We can say that the death of Socrates in ancient Greece occurred *before* this event (i.e. it was in the past at the time of Becket's murder) and the arrival of Amundsen and his team at the South Pole came *after* this event (i.e. it was in the future at the time of Becket's murder).

We can see from this example that when we refer to *past* events and *future* events, it is always with reference to some other event—the slaying of Becket in the above example. Past events come before that event and future events come after. We can also express this in terms of *moments in time*: past moments come before the moment at which Becket was slain, future moments come after.[41] We can never refer to past events and future events without reference, explicit or implicit, to some event or moment in time that we have already identified.

Think of a past experience in your life but let it be something that happened today—e.g. your waking up. Now think of a future experience, but again something that you know will happen today—e.g. your next meal. As was stated above, 'When we refer to past events and future events it is always with reference to some other event.' So in the above examples, what is this 'other event' that defines the first event you thought of as *being in the past* and the second event as *being in the future*? The answer is that it is that special moment in time that we refer to as 'the present' or 'now'. Unless we are unconscious, we all experience 'now'. Right now your experience is reading the words on this page and perhaps being aware of noises around you, objects in your peripheral vision, feelings in your body, and so on. For you, past events are those that occurred before your 'now' experience and future events are those that will occur after it.

Of course, we have already encountered this 'now experience' on our travels. It is equivalent to what in the last chapter I identified as a discrete conscious event. Every DCE is an activity of the Host—let's stick to the human brain—that occurs at a point in time in the history of the universe that is experienced as 'now' *for that Host*. Recall the image described towards the end of the last section, a universe in which there are rare, but nevertheless countless locations in

---

[41] Modern science informs us that the matter of which events occur before, after and simultaneous with a particular event is conditional on the circumstances in which these events are observed. As will become apparent shortly, this is not a relevant consideration for present purposes.

space-time at which a Host (unique to that location) engages in the activity of a DCE or 'having a now experience'. [42]

Consciousness, time and existence

Already the moment 'now' that I asked you to think about earlier in this chapter has become a past moment, and what was a future moment has taken its place. Indeed, we can say that only what is happening in your present *exists*; events in your past have *ceased to exist*, and events in your future have *yet to exist*.[43]

Imagine again those DCEs at locations in space-time, but only your own. Some are in the past and exist no longer and some are in the future and have yet to exist. Only one is in the present and can be said to exist—it's you reading these words. Hence we can see that in your subjective world, there is an intimate connection between consciousness, time and existence. The activity of your brain and nervous system and their interaction with the external world that is associated with your ongoing *conscious experience* (your DCE) defines what *exists* in your world at that *moment in time* defined as 'now'. And this activity defines what, for you, no longer exists—what is in the past—or has yet to exist—what is in the future.

At this point, you may be confused by the word 'exist' because we speak of things existing over time, not just for a particular moment in time. For example, we would agree that the desk at which I am sitting existed yesterday and last year

---

[42] The idea of a discrete conscious event as a 'now experience' is similar to that of 'the specious present'. This is defined as 'The time duration wherein one's perceptions are considered to be in the present' (see for example the Wikipedia entry for this). Thus it is not a point in time: it is of finite duration. Different forms of the specious present have been proposed of variable durations. It is not necessary for our purposes to go any deeper into this matter.

[43] The insistence that only the present exists, and the past and future do not exist, is known as 'presentism'.

and ten years ago, and I hope it will continue to exist for some years to come. This brings us back to a previous theme; you may recall that in chapter 6 I asked in what way something such as a wave in the sea can be said to be the same wave at different points in time. I raised the question whether the arguments against its being so could also apply for solid objects. I shall provide one such argument in due course.

What defines 'the present'?

Thus far, everything I have said about time and existence may seem obvious to you. But consider this: we have been talking about *your* subjective representation of time—what exists 'for you'. Does this match with what time is *in reality*? Specifically, is *your* present, the same as the *universe's* present, your past the same as the universe's past, and your future the same as the universe's future? If I say, or I hear someone say, that the universe is 13.8 billion years old, can I assume that this is *objectively* true, so that if I did not exist at all, the universe would still be at that point in its history? This is what we all assume. But could it be that where the universe is in its history, i.e. what constitutes its present, and hence its past and future, is entirely determined by consciousness? By this, I am not implying that for me, you and every other living person the universe is at different points in its history. So what do I mean? I invite you to think about this before proceeding.

CHAPTER 15

'THE PRESENT' RECONSIDERED

'Could it be that where the universe is in its history, i.e. what constitutes its present, and hence its past and future, is entirely determined by consciousness?' There are at least two routes we can go down in addressing this question, but only one of them is essential for our purposes. However, I shall mention the other route as it's the one scientists may immediately think of.

Let's consider a DCE in response to stimuli from the external environment. Pretend that at this moment you are sitting in a garden and let's 'freeze' time and consider one DCE happening 'now'. Night is falling and you can see the Moon, Venus and some stars, but it's still light enough to also see the contents of the garden—trees, bushes, plants, etc. What exists for you *now* is the brain activity associated with your conscious experience. You might include in this the activity of your peripheral nervous system, notably the responses of your sensory organs to the external world, as a result of which neural impulses are transmitted to your brain. These responses occur only a fraction of a second before the associated DCE.

Now think about what is, for our purpose, the most significant of the senses, namely vision. The receptors on the retinae of your eyes respond to photons transmitted from the various objects that are in your line of vision—the contents of the garden and what it is visible in the night sky. For you, this is how the world is *now*.[44] But, as noted in Appendix I, it takes time for light to travel from any stimulus to your eye. For the contents of the garden, this delay will be miniscule, but the further away from you the object is, the greater the delay. For the Moon this is about 1.3 seconds and for Venus between 2 and 15 minutes depending on its proximity to the Earth. What about stars? Well, the Andromeda galaxy is visible to the unaided eye and thus we see it 2.5 million years in our past.

The conclusion is that it makes no sense to say that the world we are consciously experiencing through our senses *exists now, in the present*; for any sentient observer, it is their conscious experience, mediated by the activity of their brain, that exists in a 'now moment' that is uniquely theirs.[45]

Scientists have much more to say about the absence of a fixed, universal now and the relative nature of past, present and future; but they are still able to give us the present age of the universe—the period of time since the Big Bang—as 13.8. billion years.

I have only gone down this route as far as is useful for us, as there is another, more fundamental way of addressing the question 'Is your "present" the same as the universe's present?' This does not require the scientific considerations that inform the above way of answering the question.

---

[44] Strictly speaking, much of what we 'see' is *anticipated* by our brain.
[45] You may wish to be more precise about these matters. For example, the events you observe when looking at the night sky are not happening in your 'now'. What *is* happening in your 'now' is photons hitting your retinae that have travelled from stars.

Are past, present and future universal?

Recall that in our deliberations about time, we noted that when we identify events and moments as being in the past or in the future it is always with implicit or explicit reference to some other event or moment. We specifically noted that when we refer to past and future events in our daily life we do so with reference to our immediate conscious experience, our 'now' experience or DCE. The question we are currently grappling with is why it is that this particular event, rather than any other, should be accorded the privilege of determining where *the universe* itself is in its existence, i.e. what events and moments in time are in *its* present, its past and its future. Because our understanding of time is so embedded in the way we consciously experience it, the implications of this question may prove difficult to grasp. So let's proceed slowly.

One of the premises of this book is that the world in which we live consists of the universe, ourselves included, and nothing else—no Creator separate from the universe and observing it. If there were, then this external observer could be 'keeping time' and his/her/its experience of 'now' would define absolutely where the universe is at present in its history and hence what constitutes its past and its future. (The simplest thing would be just to say that at present the universe is 13.8 billion years old; anything before this is the past, anything after is the future.)

Since I am not that external observer, when *I* refer to the universe as it is at this present moment I can only speak about my own experience, my own construction of the world. I cannot say that this is 'now' or 'the present' *in reality*, so that, regardless of whether I am alive and conscious, the universe would still be at that stage in its entire history. Neither can I say what is in the universe's past and in its future without reference to *my* 'now' experience. I assume the same is true for every other sentient being.

These assertions run contrary to our everyday thinking about the world. It seems obvious to us that there is a past, present and future that is universally fixed and independent of ourselves. Is it really the case that neither I nor anyone else can confer on the real world its own present and hence its own past and its own future? If this were so then it seems we would be forced to conclude that the universe does not have an objective 'now' or 'present' which defines what exists, what exists no longer, and what has yet to exist;[46] this is only how an individual sentient being experiences time and existence.

Discussing these arguments with others has led me to realise that they are one of the most difficult parts of the journey towards answering the questions posed at the outset. I believe that the arguments are valid but the problem is that they are completely contradicted by everyday experience. I shall therefore continue to explore this matter in detail in the next chapter.

---

[46] Another way of putting this is 'what is happening, what was happening and what is yet to happen'.

CHAPTER 16

THERE IS NO UNIVERSAL PAST, PRESENT OR FUTURE

In the previous chapter I reminded you that events occur in a time sequence so that if we consider any event, other events will have happened before it, or will happen after it, or are happening at the same time. In chapter 13 I introduced the concept of a discrete conscious experience; this is itself *a physical event* and therefore, the previous statement applies also. Subjectively, we endow this event with a unique status: we assume that it defines where *the universe itself* is in its history—i.e. its present. We take it for granted that if we did not exist, the universe would still be at that stage in its history. I have however argued that we have no reason to grant our conscious experience this status, any more than we would any other event in the universe. The present, and hence what defines the universe's past and future, is entirely subjective and personal to each one of us; it is not reality itself. In other words, time as something that determines what exists in the universe (present), what no longer exists (past), and what is yet to exist (future) is only how we sentient beings construct it; it does not have this property in the real world.

But isn't my 'now' the same as everyone else's?

Let's begin with the everyday assumption that the universe does have an *objective* present, past and future coincident with yours. Consider a specific event, namely the eruption of a certain volcano on our planet. Is this happening in the present?

Well from this information alone, you will tell me that you don't know because I haven't given you the date and time of this event. In particular, there is nothing objective that one could identify about the actual volcano and its activity that would indicate that the event is happening in the present.[47] All would be the same if this event happened in the universe's past or if it were happening in the universe's future (yes, I realise it would not be possible to witness it in that case!). Hence, one cannot as yet use this event as a reference point ('now') for identifying the universe's past and future. So how can one tell if it *is* such a reference point; what would identify it as happening in the universe's present?

Clearly one way to do this would be for you to put down this book and, assuming you could, go and look at the volcano. If you can see that it is erupting then your answer to the question will be that it is definitely happening in the present; if not it must be in the past or possibly in the future (i.e. a predicted event). Yet isn't the physical activity of your experiencing this just another event in the universe like the erupting volcano? Specifically, your brain and nervous system are reacting to light (and possibly sound) coming from the volcano and in some way giving you this conscious experience. Hence, just as I said about the erupting volcano, one can say that there is nothing objective that one can identify about *your* activity that indicates that *it* is happening

---

[47] If you were watching the event on television, without any other information, there would be nothing about the physical volcano itself or its activity that would reveal if the event were happening live or you were watching a recording.

in the universe's present. All would be the same if it happened in the universe's past or if it happens in its future. If we cannot use the activity of the volcano as a reference point ('now') for identifying *the universe's* past and future, why should we be entitled to use the activity of your brain?

What you *can* say is that both the erupting volcano and your awareness of it (your brain's activity in response to it) are happening in *your* present, *your* 'now'. But you cannot say that they are happening in *the universe's* present. That is, you are not entitled to say that the erupting volcano is an event that is occurring at the present moment in the universe's history *and this would still be the case if you did not exist.*

Does this confirm that what is the present time ('now') in the universe's history, and hence what is past and what is future, are entirely subjective and personal to you? Or have I overlooked something significant?

Once again let's suppose that instead of reading these words you are looking at the volcano, only this time you have a friend with you. 'Do you see the volcano and am I right in saying it is now erupting?' you ask your friend. 'Yes,' your bemused friend replies. Let's further suppose that there are lots of people with you and they all confirm this. Does that not reveal that, far from being personal to you, you share your 'presentness' with everyone else? Can we not say that, because everyone else tells you they are experiencing this event as happening 'now', this 'now' also exists in the real world, and thus we really are experiencing the universe at *its own* present moment in its history?

More simply, suppose you were to telephone lots of people and ask them, 'What is the time and date now?' Wouldn't they all give the same answer as you (though you may have to make adjustments for different time zones)? Like any other shared experience, doesn't this entitle you to conclude that your definition of 'the present' is indeed how the universe *really* is? In that case, how can your 'now' be entirely personal to you?

The answer is that when someone tells you what they are experiencing now, including what the time and date is, this is still only part of your own experience of 'now' just as any other event or activity that is going on around you, such as the erupting volcano in the above scenario. In other words, although you may know what other people are experiencing at the same time as you, you cannot define that as *their* 'now' or their presentness. Their reports of their experiences are events that you are experiencing in *your* 'now', just like any other event you are observing. In fact (and this is a very important point to grasp) it makes no sense even to ask whether other people's 'now', their presentness, is the same as or different to yours; they cannot be compared in this manner.

So, what do we learn from this? In the absence of any observer outside of the universe, such as a Creator, there is no absolute 'now', external to each of us, no moment or period in the universe's history that has the unique privilege of happening 'at the present time'. There is no *now* that defines what exists, what no longer exists or what has yet to exist that is independent of the observer's personal experience of now.[48]

Let's express this in terms of our concept discrete conscious event. Your DCE defines *for you* those events in the universe that *are* (now), and hence those that *were* (before) and those that *will be* (after). But there is no reason to say that this applies to the universe itself in the absence of your DCE.

From this we conclude that as you are reading these words, what has happened in your past, what is happening in your present, and what will happen in your *future*, must in some way all be 'happening together'. In more general terms, the universe itself does not have a past that no longer exists, or a future that has yet to exist: the universe exists. This

---

[48] Again I ask you to be careful not to confuse this reasoning with relativistic arguments against a 'universal now'.

doctrine of 'eternalism' contrasts with that of 'presentism' (only the present exists) as outlined in chapter 14.[49]

The space-time universe again

As an aid to understanding this conclusion, by no means unique to this book, some writers suggest thinking of time in spatial terms. Indeed, for millennia people have thought and communicated about time in this way. For example, we think of 'moving forward' in time, of periods of time being long or short, and of 'filling our time' with things to do.

Now, if I were to ask you, 'Where precisely is "here" in the universe?' you would probably tell me that 'here' is not an actual place; for you, 'here' is where *you and you alone* are presently located. Everyone else has at any time his or her own unique 'here' which for the rest of us would always be *there*. There is no fixed place in the universe itself which is here or not here; *here* and *not here* ('there') are only defined by the individual observer.

So, for present purposes, one way of thinking about time is somewhat similar to the above: consider 'now' as akin to 'here'. Like 'here', 'now' is not universal but is uniquely determined by each individual observer. 'Now' defines what exists for that observer. 'Not now' events or moments in time (past and future) do not exist *in the experience of that observer* but, in our new way of thinking, they may still be construed by him or her as happening 'over there' or 'somewhere else' in the universe.

In fact, we can simplify matters further by using the idea of space-time. We imagine a four-dimensional universe (three dimensions of space and one of time)[50]. Each and

---

[49] Unlike here, some versions of eternalism do not consider that the future exists.

[50] To get the idea, you can cheat by thinking of a universe with just two spatial dimensions—a horizontal plane—and one time dimension.

every event in the universe's entire history occurs at its own unique space-time location. Thus we have a spatial rendering of the universe as it exists in its entirety: there are no parts of it that are in the past, present or in the future.

As an aside, the concept of space-time provides one response to an unanswered question raised in chapters 9 and 14, namely whether *any* material object, such as my desk in front of me now, can be considered the same object over time. Is it the same desk that was in front of me yesterday? From a subjective standpoint the answer must be yes; nobody is likely to have come and replaced it with an identical desk while I wasn't looking! But we can argue that at a certain moment yesterday, the desk constituted 'an event' at a unique location in space-time and at its present location in space-time it is a different event. This is not to say that in the real world there is no relationship whatsoever between my desk now and my desk yesterday, but that the way our mind constructs that relationship—'the same desk'—is not the definitive representation.

Returning to our discussion of representing the universe spatially, this is akin to scientists' concept of 'the block universe'. I am going no further than presenting the above as a representation that may be more apposite than our normal way of conceiving the universe; it is not claimed that this how the universe 'really looks' which, as observed in Appendix I, is a meaningless assertion.

An analogy

To get an idea of how all of this works for our present understanding, let's consider an analogy. Imagine that you are taking a walk from your home and down your street to visit a neighbour. Even if you cannot see it, you know that your neighbour's house is there: it *exists* even before you reach it. Likewise, whether or not you turn around to look at your house, you know that it is still there: it *exists*, even though you have left it behind. Obviously when you look at your neighbour's house you are not seeing it in the future, with you standing there ringing the doorbell. And when you look back at *your* house you are not seeing it in the past, with you locking your door. The next step in this analogy is to imagine looking forward and back, seeing these two events, and thinking, 'I am *here* at my space-time location and they are *there* at their space-time locations.'

But time still exists
You will have gathered that nowhere am I claiming that time does not exist. (There are scientists and philosophers who make this assertion but I'm not sure they really mean it.) I assume that time exists in reality, and how our minds construct time is based on properties that are indeed real ('if it's on the map it's part of the territory'). Such properties, *as they are experienced by us*, include the continuity of time and its irreversibility, and the way events are related in time such as 'Event A occurs before Event B, and Event C occurs after Event B', and thus 'Event A can influence Events B and C, but Event C cannot influence Events A and B', and so on.[51] But we do not assume that these are *faithful* representations of these properties as they exist in reality. We may, however, be able to represent them more accurately if, with the help of rational thinking and scientific enquiry, we reconsider these subjective impressions.

---

[51] Rejecting the idea of an absolute past, present and future, but retaining the idea of before, simultaneous with, and after, is akin to what is termed 'the B-Theory of time' (McTaggert, 1908).

CHAPTER 17

NOW AND ALWAYS

'The universe itself does not have a past that no longer exists, or a future that has yet to exist: the universe exists.' In this chapter I shall explore further the meaning and consequences of this assertion. Before doing this I need to say that I for one find the statement so challenging that it raises a question that lies at the very heart of philosophy itself, namely what we mean by 'exist' and 'existence'. This is not an issue that concerns us in everyday life—something either exists or it doesn't—but once we start to think deeply about it, things don't appear so cut and dried. In this book we have, for example, deliberated at length on the distinction between the real world and the world constructed by the mind. You may also be aware that the discoveries and theories of modern science have challenged our understanding of 'existence'. So, to do full justice to the opening statement probably calls for a reappraisal of this concept. I am sure that you will be relieved to hear that I am satisfied there is no need to attempt this here (I'm not up to the task anyway), but I think the point is worth noting.

Let us continue with the job in hand by considering some historical figure, say Julius Caesar (100 BCE—44 BCE). For it to be meaningful to assert that Julius Caesar, at any moment in his life, or anything that he did, is in the past and no longer exists or is no longer happening, or is in the future and has yet to exist or happen, we must identify a 'now' event, period or moment in time—e.g. the second Persian invasion of Greece in 480 BCE (he is yet to exist) or the Battle of Hastings in 1066 CE (he no longer exists), or your reading these words (*ditto*). Otherwise, we can say that Julius Caesar and all his deeds, just as anything else, exist in the space-time universe. So, if I say to you, 'Does Julius Caesar exist?' you may reply 'No' if you mean he is *in our past* (before our now) or 'Yes' if you are referring to the universe in reality.

At this juncture you may wish to ask, 'How can anybody prove any of the above assertions about Julius Caesar's existence?' You may add, for example, 'I can prove that my friend exists because I am able to interact with her, but I can't interact with someone in the past like Julius Caesar or, just at this moment, someone in the future who has yet to be born. And neither can you or anyone else alive today.'

It is true that this assertion that Julius Caesar 'exists' cannot be proved scientifically, in the sense that you can prove your assertion that your friend exists. But consider the following argument: I say, 'Julius Caesar exists' while a colleague says, 'There is plenty of evidence that Julius Caesar is a real person, but also that he does not exist because he is in the past.' Now, I think I am in one sense being more scientific than my colleague: I am making fewer assumptions about the world than she is. I am not assuming that there is 'a universal present' that defines what exists and no longer exists and that happens to coincide with *my* present. I can do a good job of proving to everyone that, according to our subjective representation of the world, Julius Caesar no longer exists in the sense that all that he did is in *our* past— mine and therefore my colleague's (and yours too of course).

But I cannot prove this for the universe in reality, i.e. that he is also in the universe's past. Unlike my colleague, I make no assumption that there is an objective past, present and future that exists independently of our awareness. My colleague *is* making this assumption and, if you like, the burden is on her to 'prove it'.

I now ask you, 'What is Julius Caesar experiencing?' and quite reasonably you look at me with astonishment and say, 'What a silly question! He can't be experiencing anything, he died over two thousand years ago!' You are here speaking with reference to your 'now', which is understandable, and none of your 'now' experiences (DCEs) have occurred or will occur in the same time frame as any of Julius Caesar's! However, according to the arguments already presented, we are able to say that all of Julius Caesar's 'now experiences'— his DCEs—are happening in some region of space-time, but not one that overlaps with the one in which you or I have any of our DCEs.[52] But note that you would still be correct in saying that my question to you about what Julius Caesar *is* experiencing—meaning 'at the moment I am asking this question'—is nonsensical, because there cannot be an answer. In a manner of speaking, a*ll* of his actions, including his conscious experiences exist 'somewhere'.

Surprisingly, there is no reason why we can't say exactly the same about future DCEs including those of Hosts that for us have yet to materialise[53] (e.g. conscious beings who have *for us* yet to be born) however far ahead in the future we

---

[52] Historians often write and speak about their subject matter using the (historical) present tense, though I don't suppose this is for reasons related to the present discussion!

[53] Consider this argument: I say that, in reality, it is true that someone in my past, namely Julius Caesar, exists. Therefore we both exist. Therefore Julius Caesar can say that it is true that someone in *his* future, namely me, exists. I have no reason to assume that what applies for Julius Caesar does not apply to me also. Therefore I can say that someone in *my* future exists.

are prepared to think over the time scale that Hosts are viable in the universe. They exist somewhere in the universe.

There is more. Consider just one of Julius Caesar's DCEs: his experience of first stepping on the English shore (possibly at Pegwell Bay in Kent) on August 26th 55 BCE. (Incidentally, In Part III we rejected the idea of preservation of personal identity over time and, *as a working assumption*, attributed every DCE or 'now' experience to a unique Host and Person. This means that we ought to find an alternative way of describing the above as one of 'Julius Caesar's DCEs'. Perhaps we could refer to him as 'the Host doing the Person we all call Julius Caesar'! You'll be glad to hear that, for present purposes, unless it becomes really necessary, we don't have to go this far in our discourse in order to develop the arguments presented here; we can still do this by referring to matters in the usual way and it is easier to do so.)

Now what about your own conscious experiences, your own DCEs? Recall that in chapter 13 I asked you to imagine the entire history of the universe in four-dimensional space-time and all the DCEs that occur within it, some in the past, some happening now, and some yet to happen. But with our new understanding of time, what has just been said about Julius Caesar's conscious experiences must also apply to all *your* DCEs: those that are in your past, that which is in your present, and those that are in your future. They all, in a manner of speaking, 'are happening'—i.e. they 'exist' somewhere in space-time.

Normally you would protest that this cannot be so: 'I am only experiencing one conscious event and that's the present one. So how can all the conscious experiences that I have ever had still be happening, and who is it, if it's not I, that is experiencing all those events?' You can ask a similar question about conscious experiences you will have in the future. In fact we have already answered this question at the end of Part III, when we abandoned the assumption of continuity of personal identity.

The answer is that we are, as a *temporary* working model, considering that each of those countless events that I have termed your DCEs are enacted by 'a different Host' that 'does a different Person' and 'a different Soul'.

A film analogy

As I have done in previous chapters, it may help achieve a better understanding of the position we have now reached by thinking of an analogy from everyday life, specifically one that clarifies the assertion that all your conscious experiences exist in the universe, rather than only at that point in time you experience as 'now'. Again I remind you of the caveat that all analogies or metaphors, however helpful, have a finite range of utility.

Let's suppose that you have an old-fashioned reel-to-reel film that you took while on holiday. The film consists of hundreds of frames depicting the events filmed, and the time sequence of those events strictly follows the order of the frames from the beginning of the reel to its end. As you watch the film the frames are presented in that order; if the projector is behaving normally, the frames can't be presented in any other order (ignoring the fact that the film can be played backwards).

Now, the frames themselves exist in time *together*. When the film is in its canister, when you take it out and hold it in your hand, when you install it in the projector, or when the projector is not set properly and the film unravels and ends up on the floor, there is no ordering of the *physical frames* in time. They exist simultaneously. You can view any frame on its own as a 'now' if you put the film in the projector so that that frame is being projected as a still shot. Although it would be rather tedious, you could manually slot into the projector individual frames at random and view each one (or more simply, just hold each one up to the light). Before you do this, you could chop the film up into separate frames, jumble them all up, and pick up and view individual ones at random.

Let's stay with the last-mentioned idea. There in front of you are all the separate frames mixed up in a pile. You pick one at random, and it turns out to be a shot of you dancing in a nightclub at the resort at which you stayed. You pick up another and it is the shot you took of a plane that has just taken off at the airport prior to your outward flight. Clearly the event depicted in the first frame and your act of filming that event occurred *after* the event depicted in the second frame and your filming that. But we cannot make any such statements about the two *physical* frames that you are presently looking at.

This analogy may help you better understand our current position. We may imagine each frame of the film as being analogous to a DCE, having its own separate structure and identity. And, just like the frames of a film, we can consider that all our DCEs exist together; in neither case is there any one of them that has, *in the absolute sense*, the unique property of existing 'now', or in the universe's past or future. But we have not done away with time. The relationship between conscious experiences in terms of their *content*, as with the content of each frame in the film, must reflect 'the laws of the universe' relating to time.[54]

Meditation

We have now reached the point where I shall address in some depth the question why, if we are supposing it to be an illusion, our sense of having the same 'self' is so compelling; that is, always being **one Person** having **one Soul** associated with a constant stream of conscious experiences over time since our earliest years and until the time of our death. Perhaps before we move on you may spend some time

---

[54] Remember: 'if it's on the map it's part of the territory'. So, there is some property of the universe that is associated with our sense of the temporal ordering of events that we consciously experience. I make no attempt to speculate on the nature of that property.

considering the film analogy above. Think of all the many separate frames that, when they are in the right order, together create our experience of one unique coherent film. Then think of the relationship between the content of each frame and its neighbouring frames. Are there clues here that might help us come up with a way of answering the question we are now struggling with?

CHAPTER 18

ACCOUNTING FOR OUR SENSE OF IDENTITY

Our journey for answers to our original questions is proving to be quite an expedition and it is evident that the construct 'discrete conscious event', which I introduced in chapter 13, and its relationship with time and existence, is assuming a position of central importance. To make further progress requires us to continue exploring this and to understand its full implications. Always be aware that we are seeking more accurate ways whereby our mind may represent reality, and ways that are more useful for our purposes, but they are not reality itself ('the map is not the territory').

So let's first summarise where we stand at the moment. In chapter 13 we abandoned the idea of continuity of personal identity over time and, if only for the time being, we are considering that every DCE or 'now experience' in the universe is the activity of a unique Host. This implies that the conscious activity that you are engaging in at this moment involves one Host, the next conscious activity you engage involves another Host, and so on. Yet is appears inescapable to us that consciousness occurs as a continuous stream of related events over time and belongs uniquely to the individual we are. How are we to account for this?

A musical analogy

Philosophers and scientist confronted by the above question sometimes rely on the metaphor of listening to a piece of music. I will shortly describe my own metaphor, but first see what you make of this one without any further explanation from me.

To make it simple, let's imagine that a well-known tune is being played on a tin whistle. I'm opting for the French song 'Frère Jacques', but you are free to choose your own. 'Frère Jacques' consists of a series of notes that are played in a certain order. Now, each of these notes has an independent existence in time and the notes themselves may be played in any order at all. But barring the odd mistake there is only one order or pattern of notes that identifies the tune as 'Frère Jacques'[55]. The tune may be performed by any player, on any instrument, in any key, at any pitch, speed or volume, in any style, and so on, but we still hear one coherent, satisfying, melodious piece of music.

In *simple* terms, it is the relationship between the successive notes that gives us this experience. It is as though with anything we identify as a piece of music, each note contains a 'memory' of the notes that have preceded it and an anticipation of the note or notes to follow. But the notes themselves exist independently of the tune; it is only the listener who perceives them as belonging to one tune that is 'the same tune' throughout the performance.

Accepting again the limitations of any analogy, I invite you to consider whether the above may provide us with a way to account for our sense of continuity of personal

---

[55] Hence we laugh at the claim by English comedian Eric Morecambe that he was playing Grieg's Piano Concerto with 'all the right notes but not necessarily in the right order'.

identity over time while considering that each conscious experience we have is the activity of a unique Host.

A thought experiment

Now consider the following scenarios. Suppose you were suddenly to 'jump back in time' and, say, relive your first day in a job. How would you know that you had jumped back in time as you were having this experience? You couldn't and you wouldn't! Unlike Host [You Now], (i.e. your brain now), Host [You on your First Day at Work] (i.e. your brain at that time) would not be structured to have any explicit or implicit memories of, or be influenced by, any events that are to follow. Host [You on your First Day at Work] would only be structured to be aware of 'time present', your implicit and explicit knowledge of 'time past' prior to starting that job, and your expectation of what will be your next experience. You can apply similar arguments to the idea that you suddenly jump forward in time and live through a specific event in your future, say the day of your retirement: how would you know that you had done this *without* living through all the intervening years? The answer again is you wouldn't: nothing would be different because your brain at that point in your life would be structured to have the memories and learning that you have acquired during those years.[56]

Thus each and every Host at a point in space-time is structured in such a way that the DCE associated with it includes awareness of a historical and autobiographical context in which that DCE occurs, what we have called the activity of being that Person. It cannot be otherwise: this is what the Host is structured to do at that moment. So, for example, when you hear the telephone ring, you have the

---

[56] Again we are reminded of the exercise in chapters 3 and 4, when you imagined being your friend and your friend being you and considered the question how you would know if you were or had been successful.

knowledge of what that sound is, which room it is coming from, your feelings associated with it, what you have to do, and so on. Host [You at that Moment] is structured to do all of that. Also, each DCE includes the anticipation of what will be the DCE to follow.

Let's examine the above in more detail. Normally, a 'deterministic' perspective would maintain that at this moment, your thoughts, ideas, memories, beliefs, attitudes, expectations, actions, etc. are the result of your genetic endowment plus the totality of your life experiences up to this moment, as well your immediate environment. In this discussion I am saying, equally correctly, that it is the precise structure of your nervous system—Host [You]—that determines your thoughts, ideas, memories, etc. at this moment.[57] Hence we may ask the well-known philosophical question 'How do you know that you have not come into existence right at this moment (as opposed to, say, the moment you were conceived or born)?' In fact some scientists consider that there may be circumstances in the universe's history whereby a fully-fledged human brain, which they call a 'Boltzmann brain', could come into existence, complete with thoughts, knowledge, autobiographical memories (false of course), and so on, simply by the chance coming-together of all the necessary materials.[58] (You may be familiar with a similar theorem about a monkey eventually producing the works of Shakespeare on a typewriter.)

How *do* we answer the question of how you know you have not come into existence right at this moment? From our perspective, which does not assume the preservation of

---

[57] This is somewhat reminiscent of the nature-nurture distinction.

[58] Around 1,000 years ago, the Persian philosopher and scientist Avecenna conceived a similar thought experiment concerning the spontaneous coming-into-being of a 'floating man' and the likely nature of his conscious experiences.

personal identity, it seems that the 'you' in the question exists only for the DCE under consideration. So we may argue that it is indeed more appropriate for you to say at this moment, 'I have just come into existence' rather than 'I came into existence X years ago.' Indeed, the question seems to me to present more of a conundrum for our usual way of representing the world than the way we are representing it here, whereby we relinquish the idea of continuity of personal identity.

Now, the microscopic structure and functioning of the Host of a DCE (as usual, think of the human brain) also mediates awareness of the anticipated content of the next DCE, the content of which, in turn, will incorporate in some way the memory, including the anticipations, of the prior DCE. In the earlier example of hearing the telephone ring, this may be your intention to answer the telephone, who you think might be ringing you, whether you think the call is likely to concern something important to you, and so on. In large part there is a good match between one DCE and its content as anticipated by the preceding DCE, although unexpected events may intervene—the telephone ceasing to ring, a sudden emergency demanding priority, or whatever. Hence, to anticipate with complete accuracy the content of any DCE may require more information than that provided by the Host of the antecedent DCE, especially information about what is happening in its vicinity.[59]

The film analogy again

By now you may be making connections between what we have discussed so far and the earlier metaphor of a tune and its individual notes. But we can strengthen our arguments by making use of the film analogy from the previous chapter.

---

[59] This is relevant to the next stage of our journey when we shall challenge the mind's way of representing the world as separate objects, each being the agent of its own activity.

Consider the idea of inspecting at random single frames of the film depicting a plane taking off from your airport. Let's say there are five hundred of these and they are all jumbled up. Can you sort them into the correct order? This might be difficult but, particularly if the frames somehow encode sufficient information (not just the visual appearance and location of the plane, but its speed at that moment, its direction, acceleration, rate of fuel usage, volume of unused fuel, what is happening on board, etc.) then you could certainly make a very good job of this. This is because the circumstances and activity relating to the plane's take-off must obey strict rules, some of which relate to time: these include its speed, height, and acceleration; its position relative to stationary landmarks; and the volume of its unused fuel. These are all inter-related in a lawful manner that involves the time dimension. Thus the content of any single frame that you choose contains a sort of history of the content of the frame that preceded it, likewise for that frame, and so on, in a manner analogous to what I have described for any DCE. And just as with a DCE, the information provided by each frame anticipates in large measure the content of the one to follow.

Meditation

Let's now return to the image I described in chapter 14:

> *Think, if you can, of a four-dimensional universe in which there are rare, but nevertheless countless locations in space-time at which a Host (unique to that location) is engaged in the activity of a DCE.*

Consider now that we are thinking of this image as representing *the whole* of the space-time universe (i.e. throughout its entire history); that a minute proportion of those DCEs are what you would *normally* identify as experienced by yourself (including your present DCE); and that no part of that universe can be objectively identified as being in the past or in the future (no longer existing or yet to exist). I invite you to think deeply about the implications of thinking of the universe and conscious experience in this way, now incorporating the ideas and conclusions expressed in the present chapter.

CHAPTER 19

SOME LOOSE ENDS

I shall end this stage of our journey by mentioning two themes—one a conundrum and the other in the form of a meditation—either or both of which may have already occurred to you.

Activity at a point in time

In trying to understand how we can dispense with our everyday concepts of now and existence, I have used language and analogies that entail thinking of the universe, over its entire history, in different states that are static or 'frozen'. For example, I have invited you to think of past, present, and future experiences that you and other people have, and asked you to think of these events as somehow all existing together in the real universe. To assist this I have used certain analogies such as thinking of these events as depicted on the frames of a film. Yet all experiences involve *movement*: somebody is *doing* something or something *is happening*. Indeed, I have consistently stressed that both consciousness and self-awareness are activities and not things or objects in themselves. How then can we talk about considering any DCE as 'still existing' in some way? Unlike a material *thing*, it seems impossible to think of *activity* without it taking place over a period of time.

One way of answering this important question is to note that it is something we can also ask of our everyday ways of thinking. For example, we may say that at a certain point, an aeroplane is traveling due east at 300 miles per hour and accelerating at ten miles per second per second. (Imagine that while you are saying this you are looking at a photograph of this aeroplane in flight.) With this information we can do all sorts of calculations and make accurate predictions about the behaviour of that object. Yet how are we to understand the implication that the object is *doing* this at a particular point in space or time? We cannot visualise it as being located at that exact location while at the same time moving with a certain speed and acceleration in a certain direction.

Ultimately we need to think more deeply about these kinds of ways of representing the world, but for the time being they may still be useful and sufficient for our purposes: they still work.

A meditation on mourning

It is important amidst all our philosophical and technical discussion about the nature of our universe that we acknowledge the very profound consequences for us of what we have thus far concluded. One of the spheres of human experience for which our present discussions are very relevant is that of mourning. Nearly every one of us has been saddened by the death of a loved one, probably more than once. We miss that person and yearn to see them again. We may comfort ourselves by thinking that the person has 'gone to the spirit world' and thus continues to live (and possibly communicates with us); or that the person has gone to Heaven and we shall be seeing them again when our turn comes, unless of course our own destiny lies in Hell. We shall encounter none of these scenarios along our present journey.

What *may* comfort us is the understanding that all the experiences that the person had in their lifetime are 'still happening'. These include those experiences that involve ourselves. So we can say that the happy moments that we enjoyed with that person are still happening, still being experienced.[60]

If this is valid, then there is an obvious downside. All the unhappiness, pain, and suffering in that person's life is also still being experienced. The same goes for you and me and everybody else. We cannot say of some terrible event or period of history—famine, plague, war, genocide and so on—'their suffering is over'. It isn't and never will be.

One way to meditate on this is to think of someone who was special to you and who has died, and to think that all the conscious experiences that this person had are still being experienced by him or her—they are still happening, they are not 'here' but 'over there'. Is it comforting to you, or is it distressing? Or is it both?

---

[60] Albert Einstein may have alluded to a similar line of argument when comforting the family of his deceased friend Michelangelo Besso: 'For us believing physicists, the separation between past, present, and future has only the meaning of an illusion, albeit a tenacious one'. However, the usual interpretation of this is disputed by Rovelli (2018).

PART V

THE UNIVERSE AS ONE

CHAPTER 20

OUR NEXT DESTINATION

The model of the universe that I am presenting to you at this stage is one in which (a) every event in its entire history is located at its own unique point in space-time; (b) it has no absolute present that defines what exists, what no longer exists, and what has yet to exist, and hence all events can be said in some way to exist or 'be happening'; (c) these events include our conscious experiences; and (d) each and every conscious experience that we have, including our self-awareness, is considered as a separate physical event in space-time without continuity of personal identity.

I offer this model as a more accurate account of the world than how we normally perceive it, yet it is still subjective, a representation of the human mind. But it is not an idiosyncratic position; it is informed by ideas expounded by many philosophers and scientists (by no means unanimously). So, returning to my analogy of taking you on a journey of exploration, there has never been a stage along the way where we have been entirely alone. Far from it.

But are we any closer to answering those questions I asked at the outset: 'Why was I born the person I am?', 'What happens to me when I die?', and so on? At present it may seem that these questions are meaningless: no answers are forthcoming because the questions no longer arise. But let us not despair! We have not completed all the stages of our journey, and we need to think of the direction we should now follow which continues this process of reconstructing our everyday ways of understanding the world to bring us to a more accurate representation.

One clue as to how we should now proceed is revealed in an anomaly in the summary of our current position given above, specifically statement (d):

Each and every conscious experience that we have, including our self-awareness, is considered as a separate physical event in space-time without continuity of personal identity.

This assertion has been expressed more floridly in the following quote from philosopher Craig Callender:

We generate time's flow by thinking that the same self that ate breakfast this morning also started reading this sentence. Really there's all these different mes at all these different times. But because I think that I am identical over time, that's why time seems to flow, even though it doesn't.[61]

Although 'closer to reality', I feel that both the above ways of representing conscious experience are still too subjective: they rely very much on the way our minds represent the world, in both our thoughts and the language in which we express our thoughts. You may have already picked up my unease over this when numerous times I have qualified an assertion by expressions such as *for the time being* or describing it as *a working model*.

The 'discrepancy' that I mentioned earlier concerns something I said in chapter 13. Following our conclusions about the teleportation thought experiments, I stated:

Maybe once again we have encountered the need to distinguish our subjective and objective worlds and conclude that our overwhelming

[61] Slezak (2013)

sense of preservation of personal identity belongs to the former, not the latter.

I then went on to say:

*Note that it is not quite appropriate to express this by saying that personal identity is **not** preserved over time; rather it is more accurate to say that preservation of identity has no meaning in reality—it's a concept that we can simply ignore.*

In other words, the question of whether our personal identity continues over time in reality has no answer. Yet it seems that we *are* answering the question by saying, 'No, it doesn't.'

It appears that once again we have arrived at a point where our 'working model' has outlived its usefulness and we must set it aside. So we must now consider the question 'What direction we should now take?'

Reminiscing on a human brain

By way of preparation for the next stage of our journey, permit me to share with you a personal memory. In this memory I am holding in my hands a real human brain. I am clasping the two cerebral hemispheres so that I am looking at it from the underside. I am wondering about the person whose brain this was (though logically, can one talk about this person and their brain as though they were separate entities?). When this brain was alive it was what I we are now calling a 'Host', though of course this would have included all the peripheral nerves, the spinal cord, the sensory organs, and so on. A Host, as well as being a structure, must be able to function and thus to experience consciousness and a sense of self. Therefore, this brain is no longer a Host because it has ceased to function. Still, I fancifully imagine that in my hands I am holding this person's lifetime experiences, personality, memories, aspirations, disappointments, fears, dreams, passions, and everything else about him or her.[62]

I imagine that the person, let's say a woman, donated her brain to medical science in her will. If so, she might be a little disappointed if she knew the purpose to which it is being put. You see, it is the late 1960s and the setting is a class of undergraduate students, of whom I am one, in the Anatomy Department at University College London. We have been given the privilege of dissecting a real human brain. The class is divided into small groups, each of which has been allocated a brain that we explore using a probe and scalpel under the guidance of our tutor. We are instructed to locate each area or structure on the surface of the brain and beneath, and we hear from our tutor a little about the function of each part and its connections with other parts.

Now imagine that I pass the brain that I am holding over to you. Like me, you cradle it in your hands so you are looking at the underside. It's surprising the number of clear structures (not just ill-defined areas) that immediately reveal themselves. I point out to you the cerebellum, pons, medulla, mammillary bodies, optic nerve, corpus callosum, olfactory bulb, mandibular nerve, etc. and say something of the function of each one. Now it's your turn and you ask me, 'Which is the part that remembers?', 'Which is the part that reads?', 'Which is the part that follows directions?', 'Which is the part that regulates body temperature?', 'Which is the part that recognises faces?', and so on. And each time, I annoy you by giving you the same answer—the brain!

---

[62] This was many years before I started to contemplate the world in the radically different ways that I have described in this book. But when I now bring this memory to mind, I still think in the same way as I did then, with the same sense of awe and wonder. Whatever else—and paradoxically—this the best way for us to think and feel about these matters, the one that best suits our needs and purposes in our everyday life, even if we say it is not an accurate in reality.

Of course, I know perfectly well what you mean when you ask these questions and it is perverse of me not to give you the answers that you are obviously seeking. Clearly each structure or area of the brain is specialised to be involved in one or more functions, and it is a remarkable scientific achievement that we now have a map of these activities covering the whole of the brain. It is even possible (with the right equipment) to point to certain individual neurons and demonstrate their function—e.g. responding to movements or the orientation of lines in the visual field. However we must not lose sight of the fact that none of these parts operates in isolation: the functioning of any part of the brain and any of its nerve cells is determined by the interconnections with other functioning parts and nerve cells. In other words, everything we do with our brain is an activity of the brain as a whole (including all the sensory organs and the nerves connecting them) and not just an activity of one of its parts. Thus we can describe the brain as 'an organic whole'.

Incidentally, you might have asked me, 'Where is the soul?' The French philosopher René Descartes would have pointed to the pineal gland, which is near the centre of the brain. Descartes studied the pineal gland and described it as 'the seat of the soul' (meaning the interface between the intellect and the body). We now know that it secretes the hormone melatonin, which is important in the regulation of the sleep-waking cycle. As with consciousness, 'the Soul' as we have conceived it—awareness of self—is best regarded as an activity of the brain as a whole, although no doubt there are specific parts of the brain that are more directly involved than others.

The perspective I have taken here, when describing the brain, may be characterised as 'top-down'—i.e. starting by considering the brain as a whole, then identifying gross anatomical and functional parts (the cerebral hemispheres, the cerebellum, areas of the cortex, etc.) and working down to the cellular level. In chapter 5 I took the opposite approach—bottom-up—when describing the human nervous system (starting with the microscopic structure and functioning of nerve cells and working upwards). I shall make much of this distinction in the chapters to follow.

So why not stay a while holding and contemplating this amazing structure? Imagine it now as a living entity, an organic whole, energised and buzzing with the activity of billions of minute nerve cells firing and communicating with each other across trillions of synapses by means of tiny biochemical changes. Think of all this as an activity of the brain itself rather than lots of different activities. One object engaged in one activity. Possibly the most extraordinary object in the whole of our universe.

There are other entities, each of which we may think of as an 'organic whole' in the same way as above. A notable example is the planet Earth, and in this context the term Gaia is sometimes used.[63]

Now we come to the key question: Might we think of the universe itself in a similar, 'top-down' way: that is, represent it as one object, one organic whole, and any activity that takes place in it as an activity of the universe itself? Perhaps you would like to give this some thought before moving on.

---

[63] Lovelock (2000)

CHAPTER 21

THE WORLD OF OBJECTS

'Might we represent our universe as one object, one organic whole, and represent any activity that takes place in it as an activity of the universe itself?' Perhaps after reading the last chapter you are prepared to accept this assertion (or maybe you already did!). But you may not be convinced, and in any case some justification is required in order to make such a far-reaching claim. So let's proceed accordingly.

From chapter 6 onwards I have placed much emphasis on the distinction between objects and their activities, notably in relation to defining what I mean by Person ('something the Host does'). It's now time to re-visit this distinction and ask, 'Does this distinction apply to the real world?' Specifically, we shall challenge our everyday observation that the world consists of countless objects, each engaged in one or more activities at any time (even when they appear to us to be inactive).

More about objects
When we look around us we do indeed see a world consisting of a multitude of 'things' or 'objects' (I shall use these two

terms interchangeably). We are also able to perceive parts of objects (e.g. an area on the Moon of a particular size and shape) and identify certain of these parts as being objects ('objects in themselves'—e.g. a crater on the Moon). Although we do not think about this, there are implicit criteria that we employ for identifying parts of objects also as objects as opposed to parts that are not. For example, we are unlikely to identify an area on the surface of the moon chosen entirely at random as 'an object in itself'. It is also meaningful at times to identify an object as *not* being part of another object; for example we would normally agree that a spacecraft that has come to rest on the Moon's surface is not itself part of the Moon.

I have been talking here about our subjective world, but is all this true of the world in reality? Note that the question is not 'Do objects exist at all in the real world?'; I accept that there is *something* about the real world that is correlated with our predisposition to perceive it as consisting of countless objects ('if it's on the map, it's part of the territory') but I ask, 'Is this an *accurate* representation of the real world?' Or can we, perhaps, just say that there is only one object, namely the universe itself, and how it is divided into parts is entirely down to the observer? And can we say the same about all *activity* in the universe?

As I have done on previous occasions with this kind of question, I shall examine in depth with you the confusions and anomalies that arise when we think and communicate about the world in the usual manner (objects and their activities), and which lead us to question how accurate it is as a representation of reality.

Objects and their parts

Let us imagine that at this moment you and I are taking a walk in the countryside and I point out to you a tree that is standing alone in the middle of a field. I now ask you, 'Is that tree an object?' and, perhaps with an upward roll of your eyes, you reply, 'Yes.' Naturally, you think of the tree as a single thing, 'an object in itself'. Next I ask you the same question about one of the leaves on the tree. You have no problem in thinking of that as an object in itself, even when it is still attached to the tree. You no doubt think the same about the twig that the leaf is on, the branch that the twig is on, any other twig or branch, one of the tree's flowers or berries, any of its roots, and of course the trunk. Each of these can be considered to be 'an object in itself'. But you have also considered the tree itself to be 'an object in itself'. So how can the tree be an object in itself if everything that it is made of (down to each single cell) is also an object in itself? The answer seems to be that we can best think of the tree as one object and the leaves, twigs, branches, etc., as 'parts of the tree', even though we also acknowledge that each bit is 'an object in itself'.

But now I say, 'You tell me that any leaf is part of the tree, any twig is part of the tree, any root is part of the tree, etc., etc.; so what exactly is this object 'tree' of which you say each of *these* objects is only a part?' If you reply, for example, that by 'the tree' you mean the object that all these things combine to form, then all you are really saying when you state, say, 'This leaf is a part of the tree' is 'This part of the tree is a part of the tree'!

You may find it useful to repeat this exercise with an object of your own choice. In my case I am looking at a table and I can say that this table has four legs; this table has a smooth, shiny top; and this table has one drawer. What is this object 'table' in each of these statements and is it the same object every time? You may also choose a much larger object (how about the planet Earth?) or a much smaller object (e.g. an atom). And how about a person you know?

As you may expect, there have been lengthy, in-depth discussions and disagreements amongst philosophers as to how to address this matter[64] but it's not necessary to proceed further in that direction here. Note, however, that this business is reminiscent of those puzzles I mentioned in chapter 9 (the puzzle about when a heap of sand stops being a heap as you remove one grain of sand at a time, and the similar puzzle concerning hair and baldness). It may also remind you of the paradoxes about preservation of identity, such as replacing the parts of the ship of Theseus or Leroy's car.[65] And it will certainly remind you of the discussion we had in chapter 1 on 'the illusive I', although in that case we used different *activities* rather than different parts to illustrate the problem, something that we shall re-examine shortly.

For present purposes, the point to emphasise yet again is that these anomalies cause us no problems in everyday life, but they still belong to the world our mind constructs and how we communicate about that world. Consequently, we must think how to more accurately represent these phenomena as they occur in reality so that these anomalies do not arise.

Let's continue with the present analysis and suppose that there is a bird perched on a branch of the tree we are looking at. I now ask you, 'Is the bird part of the tree?' You would certainly say no, and I am sure we would all agree: for one thing, a moment ago the bird was nowhere near the tree, and for another, while we have been talking about this, the bird has flown away. Surely there's no confusion with this one!

Well, there *is* an issue here. In everyday life we learn implicit and explicit rules for recognising what is and is not part of any given object. So we immediately say that a leaf is part of a tree, but a bird on a tree is not. Likewise, a drawer

---

[64] A common example in the philosophical literature is the tale of a student who, after taking his parents on a tour of the buildings that comprised his university campus, was asked by his father, 'Yes, but which one is *the university*?'

[65] Thus you may ask, 'If I keep removing objects (leaf, twig, etc.) that are parts of a tree, when does the tree stop being a tree?'

is part of a desk but a plant pot on a desk is not. And so on, *ad infinitum*—I'm sure you can think of your own examples! But note that here I am no longer talking about *one* specific tree that we are looking at on *one* specific occasion. I am talking about trees *in general* (likewise desks, etc.).

As observers of the universe, we have in mind a concept 'tree' that determines whether something we see is or isn't a tree and what is and isn't part of a tree. And according to this concept, a bird sitting in a tree is not part of the tree. But 'tree' is an abstraction of the human mind and does not exist as such in the real world. We may assume that what exists objectively are billions of instances of a certain combination of features in the structure of the observable universe that give rise to recurring patterns of stimulation in our sensory systems, notably our visual apparatus. In response to an actual instance of this pattern of stimulation emanating from a particular location in space-time, information is passed via our sensory organs to the brain which then constructs 'a tree'. We can say this for anything we identify as 'an object', perhaps even the concept 'object' itself. We can also say this for anything that we identify as a part of an object. So, 'A leaf is part of a tree but a bird sitting on a tree is not' is a statement about our subjective world but not about reality.

In summary, it is not the case that it is the tree that announces itself as such to the human observer; it is the human observer who brings to this encounter the concept of tree, and amidst all of the incoming stimulation discerns a certain familiar pattern that is encoded by the brain as 'tree'; likewise 'parts of tree' (roots, trunk, branches, etc.) or 'not parts' (a bird on a branch). We have no reason to believe that any such distinctions are made by Nature except through the medium of a sentient being.

Hence, during this discussion of objects and their parts, in the present case 'a tree', strictly speaking it's best to assume that I am referring to a unique event—one particular tree that exists *in reality* at a particular location in space-time. I am not talking about trees in general or the concept of 'tree'. For the most part we can carry on the discussion without making explicit this distinction, but there will be times when we shall need to remind ourselves of this.

So what's the answer to the question 'Is a bird a part of a tree? From a subjective perspective we may persist with our answer *no*; but so far as reality is concerned, the question doesn't arise and so there *is* no answer.

As with a tree, so with the world itself. We can approach the above line of argument from the opposite direction and consider the field (an 'object in itself') in which the tree is situated and ask, 'Is this tree a part of this field?' You may shake your head and defend your response with arguments for considering the tree and field as separate objects. Alternatively, you may reason that since a lump of soil, a blade of grass, or a weed would be considered part of the field, why not the tree? After all, it grew from a little seed in the field and was nourished by the field's soil and water, along with the air around it. Perhaps we could therefore say that the tree is something that the field created; most of what it is made of has come from the field. So: no field, no tree. But again I suggest that we are arguing over a question that arises because of the way our mind constructs the world and not because of how the world is in reality. [66]

Can we extend this way of thinking to a scarecrow that we perceive in the field? We certainly can—recall our discussion of the bird in the tree—even though most people, I guess, would draw the line at including such an object as part of the field.

Now consider that this field could be part of a farm. The farm is part of the countryside, the countryside is part of an island, the island is part of a continent, the continent is part

---

[66] Note that it would seem absurd to us to ask instead, 'Is the field part of the tree?' But Nature is not offended, since neither question is relevant to the real world.

of a planet called the Earth … hold it there. Can we think of the Earth as 'an object in itself'? I think we may agree that we certainly can.[67] And surely there is no reason why we should stop there. Let's carry on and talk about our solar system and our galaxy as 'objects in their own right',[68] and, likewise, eventually our entire universe. In other words, rather than thinking of the universe as a collection of innumerable and separate things or objects, let's think of the universe in its entirety as one object, *one whole.*

Instead of the tree, we could have started with countless other examples on which to base the above line of thinking. I invite you to reflect on this using examples of your own choice. I guarantee that whatever example you choose, you will always end up by 'thinking of the universe as one object'.

What we have been examining here is how our brain performs the extraordinary feat of organising and imposing a structure on the world by identifying and processing recurring patterns of stimulation impinging on our sensory systems in ways that allow us to survive and fulfil all our everyday needs and purposes. But we cannot say that this is how the real world, as opposed to the observed world, is structured. So I am suggesting that, for the purposes of our quest, we set aside this way of thinking—i.e. dividing the world into objects—and think of the world as just one object: the universe. Of course, anything less than the universe is still part of the universe. But, for now, there is only one *object*, and that is the universe itself.

---

[67] Recall my mentioning the term 'Gaia' in the previous chapter (named after the goddess or personification of Earth).

[68] Here you may be tempted to object that, for example, individual planets in a solar system and stars in a galaxy are separated by empty space—i.e. nothing—and therefore cannot be 'objects that are parts of other objects'. But 'space' is only 'nothingness' to the human mind; in Nature, space is certainly 'something': science reveals that it is part of the fabric of the universe, seething with activity.

The world of particles

At the risk of being unduly repetitive, I ask you to consider a somewhat different way of presenting the argument that the world of objects is a construction of the human mind and not reality itself.

As you may know, scientific exploration has revealed that we can think of (i.e. represent in our mind) all visible matter in the universe, including everything that we designate an object, as being composed of configurations of the same three particles, namely electrons, protons and neutrons.[69] Configurations of these particles form the atoms of all the elements in the universe, each element having its own identifiable configuration (or configurations if you take into account isotopes). In turn, configurations of different elements bond together to form molecules. Most of what we encounter as objects in everyday life are composed of combinations of elements and/or compounds. Nevertheless we can still think of these objects as configurations of those three subatomic particles identified above. So, when I earlier talked about the human mind identifying objects from 'recurring patterns of stimulation from the outside world' I can add that these emanate from recurring configurations of particles. This is as much as we need say for present purposes about what exists in the real world (although, as always, it is still a subjective representation).[70]

Now, it requires an observer with a brain to carry out the task of carving these patterns into 'objects in themselves'. We do this automatically by using implicit criteria that are

---

[69] Scientists have discovered many other particles, and protons and neutrons themselves have been found to be combinations of more fundamental components known as ('up' and 'down') quarks. For present purposes a simplified account is all that is required.

[70] The assertion that everything in the universe may ultimately be explained in terms of the properties and behaviour of fundamental particles is one that some scientists appear willing to defend, at least hypothetically.

governed by the way our nervous system is constructed and functions, our needs and the demands imposed by our everyday environment being a major determinant of this. So here we have another way of representing the assertion that the world of objects is one our minds construct and not a true representation of reality.

The activity of objects

This, then, is the position I am arguing for: it is a more realistic, though still inevitably subjective, representation of reality to maintain that there is only one object, namely the universe itself, and not a countless number of objects. The next step is to examine the second important aspect of our current deliberations: the various activities of what the mind identifies as objects—what these objects *do*.

I earlier stated that there are implicit criteria that our mind employs for identifying what parts of an object are objects in themselves. As you have been following the discussion, it probably occurred to you that the most important of these criteria are the structure and composition of a part and how it functions, i.e. what it *does*. For example, a leaf on a tree has a very different shape from the twig to which it is attached, its material composition is different, and the two parts do different things: the leaf engages in the activity of photosynthesis and the twig transports nourishment to the leaf. We can perform a similar exercise contrasting roots, buds, blossom, berries, and so on. The focus here is on the *activities* of objects.

Meditation

I invite you now to spend some time looking around you, noticing all the different objects (including parts of objects that you identify as 'objects in themselves'). This is best done outside (thus providing you with a greater variety of objects and activities) or, if you are indoors, by including the outside world as observed through a window. Think about what it means when we say 'X *(a specific object you have identified)* is doing Y *(an activity)*. Do this for several different objects or parts of objects. (You can be quite creative, especially with objects that appear not to be doing anything at all; for instance, you can say that your chair is supporting your body or your socks are keeping your feet warm. You could even include yourself and your activity.)

Again I impress upon you that, as with the exercise of thinking about an *object* such as a tree, so any *activity* that you are considering must be one that is actually occurring in reality at a specific time and place. If you think, say, about a bird singing it must be an actual instance of this and not *the concept* of a bird singing (i.e. birds singing in general).

CHAPTER 22

THE WORLD OF ACTIVITIES

I would first like to share with you some thoughts that come to my mind when I engage in the meditation outlined in the last chapter. Amongst the events I am observing now, as a sit typing in my garden are: a blackbird is cheeping (and thus distracting one of my cats that is coming too close to its fledglings); a branch of a tree is waving; a leaf is falling from the same tree; I am lifting my hand to my ear and confirming that my watch is still ticking; the children in the garden next door are playing in a little paddling pool, and one of them, Sophie, is laughing and screaming; the Sun is shining; and a small patch of cloud is drifting across the sky. Finally I hear my telephone ringing and guess that my wife is calling me.

Why should there be any doubt that my account of these events accurately mirrors what is happening in the real world around me? Well, in the previous chapter I have suggested that considering the universe as one object rather than a collection of countless objects may pave the way for a more accurate representation of reality. If we accept this, we could say that all the activity that I am observing—the cheeping of the blackbird, the approaching of the bird's nest by my cat, the laughing and screaming of Sophie, etc.—is to be considered as activity of the universe itself and not of these individual objects that comprise my subjective world. Thus I am considering the universe to be one organic whole, one object engaged in one activity; what I perceive as objects and what they are doing are more accurately represented as bits of the universe and its activity. And I am inviting you to do the same.

At first this may not strike you as particularly profound, so we need to discuss in further depth the justification for adopting this position and the implications for doing so.

Agency and causation

Speaking for myself, when I contemplate how we represent anything happening in the world by the expression 'X is doing Y', two related concepts come to mind—agency and causation. That is, there are occasions when we represent X as the *agent* of Y, meaning that X is *responsible* for Y. For example, if I say, 'The telephone is ringing—I wonder if my wife is calling me' I have identified my wife as the (possible) agent responsible for our telephone ringing. We could also say that my wife is the *cause* of this event or even speak of her as the 'causal agent'. Alternatively, couldn't we say the telephone is the agent of the ringing? This is what I seem to be implying when I say, 'The telephone is ringing.' Some philosophers would deny this and reserve the term 'agency' for sentient beings.[71] Others may adopt a broader definition, distinguishing between 'animate' and 'inanimate' agency. In everyday conversation it does seem that we allow for inanimate agency. Some may argue that this reflects our tendency to (mistakenly) endow objects with animate properties ('I wish the telephone wouldn't keep ringing!') Personally, I find that the idea of inanimate agency does work well when we are referring to inanimate *machines* constructed

---

[71] What kind of sentient beings is a matter I shall not pursue here.

by humans—the telephone in this example. So, for the purposes of this discussion I am adopting a broad interpretation of agency.

Is agency any different from causation (so I might simply say that my wife is causing the telephone to ring or perhaps that the cause of the ringing noise is the telephone)? Again this is a matter of discussion amongst philosophers but my answer to these questions would be that it depends on what we mean by agency and causation. In other words, we are talking about matters that apply to our *subjective* world.

This now leads to the question whether our concepts agency and causation survive the suspension of our normal habit of dividing the world into objects. Or is it that they are constructions of the mind of the observer and, while they correlate with stimulation received from the external world, they are not accurate representations of it? As on previous occasions, we will address this question first by seeking out anomalies, contradictions and areas of confusion that arise from our existing understanding of these matters and then, if such are uncovered, offer a representation whereby these anomalies no longer arise.

Anomalies

Here are some anomalies that come to my mind as I engage in the exercise described earlier. I think of the general expression 'X (object) is doing Y (activity)'. I then ask myself 'Who or what is ticking, ringing, cheeping, and laughing and screaming?' and my respective answers are my watch, my telephone, a blackbird, and Sophie. Thus, each of these objects (X) is doing an activity (Y), where X is, in the broad sense of the term, the agent of Y or, if you prefer, X *is responsible for* Y.

It appears to me that two areas of confusion arise when we represent what is happening in the above terms, i.e. X *(the agent)* is doing Y *(the activity)*. One of these areas will sound familiar to you, so I'll discuss it now.

167

The disappearing object again

Take the case of my observation 'the Sun is shining'. Normally, as in the scenario I described above, this would mean something like 'The rays of light from the Sun are falling unimpeded on everything in my vicinity that is unshaded.' In other words, it is daytime and no clouds are covering the Sun. In that case, 'the Sun is shining' is not a clear statement about what the Sun itself is doing (it's very much an observer-centred description) and therefore not very useful for our purposes. Let's pretend that by 'shining' I mean the Sun's activity of nuclear fusion, whereby energy is released when the nuclei of lighter elements are forced to combine to make those of heavier elements. In the Sun, the conversion is almost entirely from hydrogen, through several stages, to helium, the two gases that account for almost all the Sun's composition. Hence the Sun is 'shining' all the time, regardless of what we observe on Earth.

I now ask myself, 'What exactly is this object we call "the Sun" that is doing the shining if "shining" means fusing small atomic nuclei to create larger ones?' Doesn't the assertion 'the Sun is shining' imply some separation between this object—the Sun—and the activity—shining—that we are attributing to it? If so, in what way can the Sun be the agent of this activity? What or where is this object 'the Sun' that is causing (or 'is responsible for') this activity of nuclear fusion?

The question I have just asked is the point I wish to make. We seem to be returning to the paradox of the 'disappearing object' discussed in previous chapter where I listed all objects that are part of a tree and then asked what is this object 'tree' of which all these objects are part. Now I have performed a similar exercise by considering the *activities* of an object (which in turn harks back to the paradox, introduced in chapter 1, of 'the illusive I', the agent of the multifarious activities which this 'I' is said to perform).

Let's pursue this further, this time using an animate object. As I sit in my garden I observe that a blackbird is cheeping. Firstly, for the sake of clarity I shall rephrase this and say that the blackbird is engaging in an activity that makes sound waves that I hear as cheeping. Now, I also notice that the blackbird is sitting on a branch but occasionally hopping or flying to a different branch; it is moving its head from side to side; it is watching my cat; we say that it is protecting its fledglings; no doubt it is breathing and exuding waste products. So again we have an object on the one hand and what the object does on the other and, as above, we ask, 'What exactly is this entity "blackbird" that is the agent of (or that is doing) all these different activities?' What or where is the 'it' that is flapping *its* wings, moving *its* head, likewise cheeping, hopping, flying, breathing, etc.?

We can continue in the present vein by considering the case of Sophie. Sophie is laughing; Sophie is screaming; Sophie is waving her arms around; she is stamping her feet; she is looking, hearing and thinking; no doubt she is sweating; and certainly she is breathing. Again we ask the question 'What or where exactly is this entity we call "Sophie", the object that is doing all these different activities?'

No problem! This question has already been answered in this book, and it is Host [Sophie], the entire physical object that we identify as Sophie, and not Person [Sophie]. Anything that Sophie does is done by Host [Sophie], including *being* that person we know as Sophie.

But oh dear! We have just discovered that there are problems with our habitual way of identifying objects and what these objects do. (Note also that, just as we asked the question 'What is this 'tree' of which each of these *objects* is a part?' we may ask the same question about Host [Sophie] and indeed the blackbird in the previous example).

I have maintained all along that, while not making much sense according to our usual way of understanding the world, thinking of the Person we are as something our Host does brings us closer to a realistic representation of the world. But

169

the questions we asked in the previous paragraph reveal that we can only go so far with this before we uncover problems that demand a new way of thinking, or at least some modification of our existing thinking. I assure you that we are heading in this direction, albeit at a slow, steady pace.

What defines the agent?

We now come to the second area of confusion I alluded to earlier, by considering the case of 'X is doing Y' when X is 'a leaf' and Y is 'falling' Is the leaf the agent of this activity? You will probably reply that it is the leaf that is doing the falling—no doubt about that—but you would probably deny that it is the *agent* of—i.e. responsible for—the activity. When a leaf falls from a tree it's not really engaging in an activity; it is responding passively to the gravitational attraction between itself and the Earth.

Similarly, let's think about my observations that the branch of a tree is waving and a cloud is drifting across the sky. Is the 'X', the object in each of these statements, the agent of Y, the activity? I think you would say no; but then what is? The wind of course. Is the wind an object? No, wind is air moving between areas of different atmospheric pressure. So now we are speaking about *causation*: differences in air pressure are causing the wind which, in turn, is causing both the cloud to move and the branch to wave. A difference in air pressure is not an object of course, so we must now ask what is causing this difference. You may come up with an answer, but at this point it may be apposite to remind you that we are not dealing with the general case but the actual event that I am witnessing right at this moment. If you know more about meteorology than I do you may answer the question by speculating in general terms, but other than that, you have no information that will allow you to address the specific instance I am observing now.

What about my noticing that my watch is ticking? This is a bit more complicated than the cases of the leaf, the branch and the cloud. If you were to ask me (improbably), 'What is making that ticking noise?' the best answer I can give you for everyday purposes is 'It's my watch.' But if you asked me to explain this further, as with with the blackbird cheeping I would say that the *activity* of my watch is making sound waves that we hear as ticking.

Can we then say that the watch is the agent of *this* activity? Or is there no difference between my watch doing this and the examples of the leaf, the branch and the cloud which, even under my broad definition, we don't consider to be agents of their respective activities of falling, waving and drifting? Just as we say that the leaf's falling is a response to gravity and that the movements of the tree and cloud are responses to the wind, could we not say that my watch's ticking is a response to the energy emanating from the battery that has been placed inside it? If so, what has happened to the concept of agency in the expression 'X is doing Y' where X is my watch and Y is the activity 'ticking'?

Can we address the same questions to the blackbird cheeping and Sophie laughing and screaming? We earlier agreed that, unlike the falling leaf, the swaying branch and the drifting cloud, the blackbird and Sophie are each the agent of the activities we observe. But is there any difference in reality? Can we not simply say, as above, that just as the leaf's falling is a response to gravity and the movements of the tree and cloud are responses to the wind, the blackbird's cheeping is a response to the presence of its fledglings and my cat, and Sophie's laughing and screaming is a response to her brother splashing her with water?

Well, I think that at the moment you are entitled to say to me: 'OK, so in the ways we represent our world we have differences in interpreting various events where we say, "X is doing Y" but it seems to me that you are just playing around with words.' But the key questions are these: 'Do such differences exist in reality and if so, what are the implications?'

To take this further we need to explore in further detail our everyday observation that events 'cause' other events to happen.

CHAPTER 23

AN EXPLORATION OF CAUSATION

Causation is a concept that we use much of the time to understand and explain our experiences. We also implicitly understand the association 'cause and effect'. For example, we may say that the ringing of the telephone is an effect due to my wife dialling our home number on her mobile phone; in turn the ringing is the cause of my lifting the receiver (an effect).

We must also be mindful that scientists themselves have studied in great detail the mechanisms of causation for a multitude of phenomena and are able to provide explanations for how these phenomena occur when these are not so obvious to us. Scientists also inform us that there are strict conditions under which causation operates. For example, contact in space-time must be preserved between the elements involved, so that for X to affect Y, something must happen or exist in the space and time that separates them, with no gaps. There is also a constraint related to the speed of light or any electromagnetic radiation: we cannot have instantaneous cause and effect, so something happening on a star 100 light years away cannot cause events to happen on the Earth for at least 100 years, since nothing travels faster than light.

One important property of causation, clearly evident in our everyday lives, is that we cannot have backward causation in time, however we conceive of time.[72] For example, an earthquake that happens in California today cannot have caused the ground to tremble in that state the previous year; and if, while I am sitting in my garden, a cloud suddenly covers the Sun, the resulting drop in temperature can only happen *after* that event and not before.

So it does seem that there is a special kind of relationship between certain events in the real world that we can designate 'cause and effect'. By this we mean that the events are connected in a way that obeys certain laws relating to time and space, and scientists can provide explanations for how the two events are causally linked. These explanations imply that if event X causes event Y, X is essential for the occurrence of Y; if event X had *not* occurred, event Y would not have occurred either (here meaning 'occurred in the exact way that it did'). So if, in the earlier example, the cloud did not cover the Sun, the ambient temperature would not have dropped in the way that it did.

Multiple causation

There is one further aspect of causation that is central to how we shall proceed. I began talking about this when I was considering the causal events behind the branches swaying and the clouds moving. Causation is not a simple linear process—a single chain of individual events and their causes—although it's often convenient to think of it in that

---

[72] Here, despite the conclusions of the earlier chapters on this matter, I am speaking about time in the manner that our mind normally conceives it. There is no risk of any contradiction between those conclusions and the present discussion of causation, since the former acknowledge that the relationships 'before' and 'after' do exist in some form in the real world.

way. Any single event is the outcome of a multitude of other antecedent events and conditions in combination. Hence, each of these events is necessary but not sufficient for the former event to occur in exactly the way it did.

With all these considerations in mind, let us start to address those anomalies and questions that arise when we represent the world by the formula 'X *(an object)* is doing Y *(an activity)*'. Recall that our aim is to arrive at a way of representing reality whereby these anomalies do not arise (rather than to discover true answers to the questions they pose). In fact I have already indicated in chapters 20 and 21 what our destination will be, but it is important that this does not prejudice our reasoning. I ought also to say here that that the arguments I am about to deploy are based on highly deterministic assumptions.

To fulfil the above aim, it is now essential that we stick rigorously to the rule that when we are talking about a leaf falling, a watch ticking, a blackbird cheeping, and so on, we are considering each as an actual event that occurs at specific and unique location in our space-time universe. We are also considering the event *exactly* as it occurs. By this I mean that once we consider the slightest variation in when, where and how it occurred then are no longer considering the same event: it is a *different* event. Unless we adhere strictly to this rule, we cease talking about the real world. It's that simple. This injunction has not been as important to the present discussion up until now, and I have been able to speak about the occurrence of the events in question and their causes in general terms, that is at a conceptual or abstract level. But we must now endeavour to strip away our subjective ways of representing world as much as possible and contemplate what remains.

So let's put our plan into action by first using the example 'my watch is ticking'. This has to be really happening, so let's make the event just a few ticks of my watch—not any ticks, but only these particular ticks. We assume that my experience of what I identify as my watch ticking correlates with *something* that is happening in the real world at a unique location in space-time but does not duplicate it. I might now ask, 'What has caused this event that my brain represents as my watch ticking, to occur?' However, this question is still too firmly rooted in our way of thinking of the world in terms of cause and effect. Let's ask a more general question: 'How do we account for the fact that at this unique location in time and space, this particular event has occurred?'

According to our mind's representation of the world, a reply to the question 'What is causing my watch to tick?' might describe the watch's mechanism and the role of the battery in generating the energy required for the ticking activity to occur. But rephrase the question as above and the answers appear to be limitless. If we just consider the location and timing of the event (which I shall refer to as 'the token event' when clarification is needed) then the wrist on which I wear my watch has to be *precisely* at the time and place it is *in the universe* in order to account for the event in question: if it were elsewhere in the universe, at however so small a distance, it would not be the same event that we are considering[73]. Thus the particular space-time location cannot be considered as separate from the event. It is part of it. And for my wrist to be there, the rest of me must be present as well! Therefore I have to be doing precisely what I am doing for the token event to occur. The watch must also be present of course; not any watch, but *this* watch. I therefore had to choose *this* watch the last time I went to buy a new one. Incidentally, the battery ran out a while back, so accounting for the token event must include my installing a new battery.

---

[73] Admittedly there is uncertainty about what constitutes 'an event' with reference to its temporal and spatial extensions (how long it lasts and how much space it occupies). I shall discuss this matter in due course.

This discussion could take forever, because for any event that we say is necessary for the token event to occur, certain events also needed to have occurred, and we can say the same about *those* events, and so on and on. For example, someone would have had to have made the watch, and someone would have had to have made me!

You may have realised that we have arrived at a place we have already visited on our travels. Recall in chapters 6 and 7 the meditation on 'the unlikeliness of me' and our subsequent discussion of 'the unlikeliness of anything'; the occurrence of any event that actually happens depends on so many other conditions being in place that we may argue (erroneously) that it's astonishing anything happens at all.

You may find it more than a little bizarre that our answer to the question 'What is causing my watch to tick?' includes reference to how my watch and I came to be in the very place that this event is occurring and how both came to exist at all. Recall once again that in everyday life, when we refer to 'my watch ticking' we are normally speaking in conceptual terms, and it would indeed be bizarre to include the above events in our causal explanation. In reality, however, 'my watch ticking' can only refer to an actual event that occurs, if it occurs at all, at a unique location in space-time. Indeed, as I earlier stated, its actual location in space-time is part of the event. Therefore our discussion about what is causing this event becomes a discussion about what is necessary *in the universe* for this event to occur. There will be many events which my mind (and anyone else's) represents as 'my watch ticking' but each occurs at its own unique location in the space-time universe; hence a unique account of its occurrence is required. This is so because Nature, in a manner of speaking, doesn't just select those conditions that are apposite for how this event is represented by the human mind—the watch's mechanism and how the battery functions—and disregards everything else; we have no reason to suppose that Nature makes such distinctions.

Let's now apply this analytic approach to an event involving a human being, in this case little Sophie. (Note that although I am making the case for rejecting the notion of a universe of objects and their activities, for the present I am adhering to this way of representing the world to explain my arguments. Eventually we shall have to consider how the world may be represented otherwise.)

What is causing little Sophie to laugh and scream? The immediate ('proximal') cause is her brother splashing her with water and this is the reply that those present would certainly give. And if Sophie's parents wish her to cease making all this noise, they would no doubt tell her brother to stop throwing water at her. But now we consider that what is occurring is an event that is happening at a unique location in the space-time universe and start to think of all the events and conditions that will have to have occurred or be in place for *that* event to happen—their father filling the paddling pool with water; the weather being sufficiently warm and sunny; the parents deciding to spend time in the garden; their decision to buy the paddling pool in the first place; and so on.

What about 'Sophie being born' and 'Sophie's parents meeting'? By now I think you know how to address these questions, including how to explain why they are appropriate for present purposes but entirely at odds with how we normally represent our world.

Incidentally, under normal circumstances Sophie and her brother would be attending school, but this event is occurring during the Covid-19 lockdown; thus this miniscule coronavirus that originated in China is part of the causal network! (And what caused the increase in the amount of cardboard left outside our neighbours' houses for recycling at this time? The coronavirus again! People were relying more on home deliveries during the lockdown.)

There is more to follow on this theme. What we identify as the effect of this multiple-causation process extends into the future, like ripples on a pond. Sophie's laughing and screaming is having an effect on you right at this moment! Maybe you can think of all the things that needed to have happened between Sophie's laughing and screaming at that moment in the past and its affecting you now. And, albeit probably in the minutest of ways, it will continue to have effects on you in the future.

So far, so good

I hope by now that you are seeing a picture emerging that may allow us to consider that the objects that I have used in my examples above may be more accurately represented as parts of one larger structure, the universe itself, and their respective activities as part of one activity, that of the universe itself. However, there is more work to be done on this theme before we arrive at the point where I can assert this with due confidence. This requires that we explore in further detail the premise that the essence of a causal agent, X, of any event, Y, is that without X, Y would not occur in the way that it did.

CHAPTER 24

MORE ON CAUSATION

I have no interest in golf and maybe you don't either, but I am choosing playing golf as an example that will further our discussion of the world of objects and activities. As previously, the arguments to follow only apply to a real event, one that occurs at a specific location in time and space in the real world.

Consider the activity of teeing off[74] during a round of golf by someone we shall Mrs A at a certain time and place. Now, in order for the ball to go soaring over the fairway (event Y) it is necessary that Mrs A first swings her club and hits the ball (event X). Y, the token event, would not happen if X did not occur, so we understand that X is the cause of Y. Moreover, our understanding of the world is that since X has to precede Y in time, Y (the ball soaring down the fairway)

---

[74] Remember that according to how this discussion is progressing, it is the human observer that identifies this activity as a separate event ('teeing off'). In the absence of this it is just part of the activity of the universe, without any unique significance. So this is not a discussion about 'teeing off' in general, nor will it say anything about this activity that may be of use to golfers!

cannot be the cause of X (the club striking the ball)—we cannot have backward causation in time. Hence we have no problem identifying which is the cause and which is the effect. But is it as simple as this? I'll return to this question shortly.

For the moment, let us think briefly about all the other antecedent events and circumstances that would need to have happened or been in place for the token event Y to occur at this point in space and time. I have already illustrated this way of thinking when we considered the paradox of 'the unlikeliness of anything' in chapter 7 and the examples of my watch and Sophie above. Therefore I don't think it's necessary to spend much time on this now; indeed we could take forever doing so, since we don't have merely to stick to those prior events and all their nuances that may have occurred during the round of golf in question. 'Planning permission by the local council to build the golf course' has to be a factor, not to mention 'Mrs A's parents meeting, falling in love, marrying', and so on and on. Eventually we will be asking questions such as, 'How did planet Earth come to be in this condition at that time?' and 'How did planet Earth come to be in existence at all?'

Can we be even more radical than this? Let's think about just *any* event that takes place prior to the tee-off—say someone in the clubhouse ordering some sandwiches. No one would seriously suggest that this action has anything to do with the behaviour of the golf ball in question! But consider this: in order for just one thing to be different—the man *not* ordering some sandwiches—lots of other things have to be different too, likewise for each of *those* things, and so on and on—*an endless cascading series of events*. Thus, had the man not ordered some sandwiches, we would be in a different universe to the one we are in now (because in *this* universe he did). Hence we may argue that in our universe the man ordering sandwiches in the clubhouse and the golf ball flying down the fairway *must both happen* in the exact manner each of them do. Now you may begin to see how seemingly unrelated actions are both part of an interdependent network of events extending over time and space and ultimately the universe itself.

Let's return to the matter of insisting that in a cause-effect relationship (1) the effect (golf ball flying down the fairway) cannot occur without the cause (golf club hitting ball), but (2) it is *not* the case that the cause cannot occur without the effect. Is this really true? Well, surely, in order for the club to hit the ball *in the exact manner that it does* it **is** necessary for the ball to go flying off down the fairway *in the exact manner that it does*. If it doesn't, then the club cannot have struck the ball in the precise manner that it did! Therefore event X, the precise cause, cannot occur without event Y, the precise effect.

Well, it would be indeed presumptuous of me to dispute a fundamental law of science, not to say everyday observation and reasoning. And I am not doing so; what we call the laws of causation do reveal significant truths about the workings of the real world. Nevertheless, they are still based on how our sensory apparatus and brain react to and process information from the external world; they are not reality itself.

The butterfly effect

All the arguments I have deployed in my analysis of cause and effect may be brought to bear in the case of a more illustrious, though hypothetical, example in which cause and effect are more remotely separated in time and place than in the example above. It is said that by flapping its wings at a certain time and under certain terrestrial conditions, a butterfly in Brazil could cause a tornado in Texas.

This sounds very profound and impressive—and I, for one, think it is. Although it is not possible to prove something as large-scale as this, I have confidence in scientists who maintain that, according to what they know about the dynamics of any system with interrelated parts, it is possible for miniscule variations involving a minute component to have far-reaching effects involving the entire system. This may make it impossible for them to predict the exact status and behaviour of the system at any point in the future, though they may still adhere to a deterministic doctrine.

I think we should spend some time wondering whether it is true *in reality* that this butterfly, merely by flapping its wings, can cause such havoc thousands of miles away. I suggest that this is the mind's way of representing this scenario and that our concept of 'cause' does not represent the real world with complete fidelity. It seems to me (and others share this view) that 'the butterfly effect' is a *reductio ad absurdum* of our concept of 'causation'. By this I mean to suggest that, like so many ideas, it has a certain range of convenience beyond which its limitations become apparent and a reappraisal is necessary. So, as is our wont, let's ask some challenging questions.

This is where the previous arguments about teeing-off stand us in good stead. As has been noted, we may construe any element of a causal network as itself the outcome of a causal network going further back in time. So let's ask, 'What caused the butterfly to flap its wings exactly at the time and place that it did?' One contributing factor could well be the local weather conditions. Then we may say, 'The weather in Brazil influenced the weather in Texas.' Not so impressive now. And this is just one of many answers that we could give.

Is there an obvious repost to the above? The scenario I have just described depicts the weather in Brazil as having an influence locally (causing the butterfly to flap its wings) and remotely (causing the tornado in Texas). In *that* scenario you may argue that there is no *causal* connection between the butterfly and the tornado. However, I have overlooked the obvious implication in the original example, namely that, regardless of what caused the butterfly to flap its wings, had it not done so, the tornado would not have occurred, or a tornado would have occurred that was different in some way—in time, energy, location, duration, etc. The butterfly's actions were, among many other things, essential to the manner of the tornado's occurrence.

So now we ask the question 'What could have happened to *prevent* the butterfly flapping its wings?' Suppose a bird suddenly swooped on the poor insect and ate it before it could perform this action. In that case we might say that, thanks to this bird, the tornado in Texas would not occur in the way that it would otherwise do. But, as we argued before, we can't just change one thing and nothing else: for the bird to swoop, lots of other conditions in the extended causal network would have to be different, so again we are talking about a different universe.

Surely the tornado wasn't inevitable after the flapping of the butterfly's wings, since other events were at liberty to occur which would result in no tornado? The same argument applies as above; for anything to be different, so many other things—and these will include those extending back in time—have to be different too.[75] Can we argue, therefore, in the same manner as for the tee-off, that the tornado in Texas (assumed effect) must take place for the butterfly to flap its wings (assumed cause)? The answer appears to be yes.

So, what do we conclude from this?

(i) We accept the scientists' claim that it is possible for the flapping of a butterfly's wings in Brazil to be connected in some way (I am now avoiding the term 'cause' here) with the later occurrence of a tornado in Texas.

---

[75] The problem again appears to be that counterfactual arguments ('If X hadn't happened what would have happened regarding Y?') run up against the reality that the universe in which the events in question occur *has* to be the way it is.

(ii) Let us suppose that it has been proved that this is indeed the case for an actual butterfly and an actual tornado—we are no longer speaking hypothetically.

(iii) The mind's way of interpreting the above, namely as two separate events with a cause-and-effect relationship (the butterflies actions *cause* the activity of the wind to behave as a tornado) does not accurately represent the real world. To bring us closer to a more accurate representation, we think of the two material structures—butterfly and tornedo—as parts of a larger structure or system, the universe itself, and their respective activities as part of one activity, again that of our universe itself. Thus they are related by necessity: one does not occur without the other.

(iv) We may apply this thinking to any actual events in our universe that we interpret as causally connected.

Yet again I feel the compulsion to stress that these arguments only apply when we are considering a specific event in the real world. It would be incorrect to say that, as a general rule, tornados are related to the flapping of a butterfly's wings thousands of miles away, or that the movement of golf balls at tee-off are associated with a person in the vicinity ordering some sandwiches. Scientists provide us with explanations of what causes air to form a tornado or a ball to move in the manner it does when struck by a hard object, and in neither case do they involve, respectively, the wings of a butterfly or the ordering of sandwiches. From the standpoint I have taken, I maintain that the scientists' accounts, and indeed those of people in general, *are* based on what happens in reality, but they are still coded reconstructions of the observer's sensory apparatus and brain. They rely on abstractions—tornados, balls being struck, etc. *in general*—which do not exist as such in the real world. Recall that by 'abstraction' I am referring to the process of observing and classifying regularly occurring patterns of sensory stimulation as particular kinds of objects involved in certain kinds of activities. These objects are observed to relate to one another in ways that are recognised by the human mind as lawful and predictable ('Event A ["cause"] always precedes event B ["effect"]' and so on). However, for our purposes we are not analysing the world according to how the human mind perceives it. What exists in the *real* world are not abstractions but individual—i.e. unique—events occurring at unique locations in space-time. And what we have been exploring here is how the occurrence of one such event—and I mean occurring in the exact manner that it does and at that exact space-time location[76]— relates to any other event in space-time. For such purposes we need not concern ourselves with the distinctions cause and effect.

Summary

This has proved to be a rather tortuous stage of our journey and if you found yourself getting a bit lost, don't worry; we are heading towards a much-simplified way of thinking about the universe. At this point we have merely set aside our normal way of representing the world as a collection of separate objects and their activities, and we now consider there to be only one object 'in reality', namely the universe itself; what we normally perceive as objects or things we simply consider to be 'parts of the universe' and any activity that we identify we consider to be an activity of the universe. This activity has a definite structure and is subject to strict laws governing how the occurrence of any event relates to events that precede it in time (what the mind identifies as the causes of that event) and events that follow it (what the mind identifies as the effects or consequences of that event).

---

[76] This is an important qualification. The non-occurrence of event A (e.g. the flapping of the butterfly's wings) may be associated with the tiniest difference in, for example, the location and timing of event B (the tornado), but by virtue of this we can say that B is now a different event.

However, when we are considering just one actual event, we simply regard the before and after events as associated with it 'by necessity'.

One final point to note. I am continuing to acknowledge that the properties 'before' and 'after' exist in some form in reality, while insisting that they are always relative to whatever event in space-time we are considering. Nothing I have stated contradicts the assertion that there is no objective past, present and future that identifies where the universe is in its history nor what in reality exists, has ceased to exist, or has yet to exist.

CHAPTER 25

POSTSCRIPTS

There are a few loose ends and afterthoughts that are worth mentioning before we move on to the next stage of our journey.

Events

You will have noticed that for some time I have been making increasing use of the term 'event'. By 'an event' I mean what is happening at any location in the space-time universe and includes the space-time location itself. Thus we may think of the universe in terms of myriads of interconnected events occurring in space-time.[77] Recall that we can say that every location in space-time is unique, and likewise, of course, the associated event. For practical purposes 'location' means something more substantial than a point; the events I considered in the last chapter have extension over time and space. Thus there is uncertainty about what constitutes 'an

---

[77] There is nothing original about this. The theoretical physicist Carlo Rovelli (2018) argues that the universe is made up of 'events' or 'happenings' and not 'things'.

event' with reference to its temporal and spatial extensions This uncertainty is inevitable because 'event' as used here is still a subjective construct and I have difficulty conceiving exactly what it represents in reality. I am confident that the arguments presented in this section of the book can tolerate a degree of vagueness or flexibility in the way this term is used without compromising the validity of the conclusions.

Postscript on the 'butterfly effect'

In anticipation of matters that will come up later in our journey, it is apposite here to explore another aspect of 'the butterfly effect'. I have suggested that it is possible for the occurrence of an actual event of the magnitude of, say, a tornado and a tiny event, such as the flapping of a butterfly's wings to be mutually necessary in our universe. But on the scale of an object the size of a butterfly, flapping wings are 'a major event'. So what kind of 'tiny event' has a relationship of mutual necessity with *this* 'major event'? One answer is that within the butterfly itself there will be biochemical changes at the molecular level, the prior occurrence or non-occurrence of which will be related to whether or not the butterfly flaps its wings at any particular moment (which in turn is related to whether or not a tornado occurs thousands of miles away). Thus we can talk about 'activity of the universe' even at these microscopic levels.

We can extend this way of thinking to human behaviour. Every activity, great or small, that any human being does, has done, or will do is mediated by the minute molecular activity in his or her nervous system (see chapter 5). Without it, we do nothing. I think this is very significant, especially when it comes to delving deeper into the status—in the real world—of what I have called 'a Host'. But more of this later.

Another thought experiment

There is a further meditation or thought experiment that complements the discussions in the present section. As it is not essential for understanding our present position and as I am anxious not to overburden you with the details, I think it is safe to leave it to you to study this now or later or not at all. Accordingly I have placed it in the Appendix (Appendix III). I have called it 'The Body, the Mind and the Universe', and it is a variation on the theme of the exact replication of a human brain.

How are we to conceive of the universe now?

I have argued in previous chapters that the world of objects or things and the activities in which they are engaged is a construction of the human mind and not an accurate representation of reality. In support of this I cited various conundrums that arise when we make statements such as 'This is X', 'Z is part of X', and 'X is doing Y'. Analysis of such statements reveal that what we mean by X (a tree, an individual person, 'me' and 'I', etc.) is deceptively elusive, although this doesn't usually give us any problems in everyday life. (Recall the earlier hypothetical example of the parents who asked their son, after he had taken them round his university campus, which building was the university.) So when I say that all activity is an activity of the universe, doesn't that still leave us with question 'What do we mean by the universe?'

The answer is to keep in mind that we are considering the universe as one organic whole. Everything we recognise as an object is simply part of that one universal object, likewise every activity. Our next task is to find a useful way that our mind can envisage all of this. Remember that we are seeking a more accurate way of representing the real world than how we normally do for our everyday purposes, but whatever we come up with can never be 'the real thing'.

You may prefer to choose your own image or analogy. What comes to my mind is the universe as a vast, heaving ocean. Maybe you could try thinking of it in this way now and see if it works for you. As I have said several times, all analogies have their limitations: in real life our considerations of the composition, structure and behaviour of an ocean must take into account 'the non-ocean'—e.g. the land, the atmosphere, and other terrestrial, as well as extra-terrestrial, conditions. But it will do no harm here to think of this ocean as like a universe—i.e. 'it is all there is'. Our task is to describe it as it is and not as an observer would see it—logically impossible of course, but we can approach this goal.

My immediate thought is that all the activity of this ocean is interconnected in some way. It is not random: it is patterned in a lawful manner ('lawful' here referring to 'the laws of Nature'), at every magnitude of scale. At the macrolevel there are huge surges, storms, tsunamis and tides; at the microlevel there is constant motion, including regular and repetitive movements at the periphery that we call waves and wavelets. We may think of the ocean as ultimately composed of the same fundamental materials throughout, but within the ocean there will be lawful (non-random) variations in the way this material is arranged and behaves. For example, the chemical composition of the ocean will vary at different locations, as will its energy, temperature and density, and these properties will be shifting continuously.

Some of these variations may be of such a nature that in certain locations material is able to self-replicate. From this, life may emerge of increasing scale and complexity in the form of what we identify as unicellular organisms all the way up to those we call, for example, 'fish'. But *crucially* let us avoid this delineation of substance and behaviour with reference to *entities* that *do* certain activities. In other words, let us not put a boundary around the activity and identify the material thus enclosed as the 'object' that is the performer of this activity—a fish is swimming, an octopus is grasping its prey, a whale is diving, etc. Instead lets us think of these and any other localised 'events' as areas of activity of the ocean itself, recurring interconnected patterns in the way its material is arranged and behaves. Now imagine our universe and all the objects in it, including human beings on Earth and other life forms, in an analogous manner.

The above way of imagining the universe adheres to our usual way of thinking about time. Ultimately, we may think of this ocean with its entire history represented in four-dimensional space-time, as we considered in earlier chapters. But perhaps more importantly, notice that in the illustrations I have been using throughout this section, you and I are acting as onlookers; we do not explicitly include ourselves among what we listed as being parts or bits of the universe, and we did not include our own activities as being part of the activity of the universe. We are not entitled to grant ourselves such a privileged status. You and I are indeed 'bits of the universe', and anything that we do is an activity of the universe as a whole.

This is something we need to think about more deeply. Most notably, we need to examine the implications of considering what I have defined as Host [You], the physical you, as being a part of the universe and all that Host [You] does as an activity of the universe. Recall that this includes the activity I have identified as Person [You] and this includes 'awareness', 'consciousness' and 'a discrete conscious event'. Consider also the activity I have labelled Soul [You], your awareness of being (i.e. doing) Person [You]. What are the implications of considering all of these as activities of a larger organic whole, namely the universe? I invite you to consider this before embarking on the next stage.

PART VI

THE THEORY OF THE SOUL

CHAPTER 26

THE UNIVERSAL HOST

Our present position, represented by our oceanic metaphor, is a dramatic simplification of how we usually think about the world. Whereas in normal discourse, and indeed in this book, we cannot avoid talking about objects and their behaviour, we are now considering the universe as one object and all things in it as parts of that organic whole. We are also taking the stance that any activity (any 'event') that occurs at any location in space-time is an activity of the universe.

Human beings themselves are parts of the universe; therefore anything a human being does is an activity of the universe. This applies to any activity of our body, including our brain and nervous system. This activity includes being (i.e. doing) the Person we are and hence all activities represented in consciousness—thinking, feeling, imagining, remembering, dreaming, etc.

It also includes the activity we have identified as awareness of being the Person we are, i.e. the Soul. I have up until now identified all of these as activities of the physical object I have called the Host and it will be more convenient for us if I continue doing so for much of the time. But keep in mind that ultimately we are considering any Host to be, not 'an object in itself', but a part of the universe, and anything we say that it does is an activity of the universe.

So we can now take a crucial step and state the following:

> *The composition of our universe is such that at certain locations in space and time it is consciously aware of its own structure and activity; this includes awareness of being aware of such.*

Normally, insofar as this proposition applies to human conscious experience, we would equate the 'locations' in the above statement with the human brain and we would say it is this object that 'does' the activity associated with consciousness. Are these two ways of thinking about consciousness contradictory? I don't believe they are and I think it's important to explain why.

The 'top-down' and 'bottom-up' approaches

Theories that attempt to explain consciousness usually rely on scientific investigations of the structure and activity of the human brain, down to (and indeed below) the level of the nerve cells themselves. As I have said in earlier chapters, it is reasonable to consider that the property of consciousness has something to do with the sheer complexity of the brain and the unimaginable number of interconnections involving the billions of units of which it is composed.

When we adopt this approach, we think of the brain (or Host in our terminology) as an object separate from the rest of the universe, although of course it is still part of it. More generally, we conceive of a set of objects in the universe that have the property of being Hosts and a set of all other objects that do not have this property. I have previously referred to this as the 'bottom-up' approach because the starting point is the brain and its individual neurons and neural networks, and we ask how this object is able to be aware of its external world as well as itself and its own activity.

The bottom-up approach is crucial in order to arrive at a full understanding of the phenomenon of consciousness. But I do not think that it alone will provide the answers to the questions posed at the beginning of our journey—the questions about the Soul and its fate.

At this stage of the journey, I refer to the approach I am arguing for as 'top-down'. That is, we think of a Host, such as the human brain, as part of the universe (and a minute part at that) and we simply consider the universe as one object, and any activity, including 'being a Host' and being consciously aware, as activity of the universe itself.

To support the above proposition, we need to apply the same analytical approach illustrated several times in the previous section for objects and their activity, on each occasion using an actual event that occurs at a unique location in space-time—my watch ticking, the golfer teeing off, and so on. It will be instructive to go through this process for a conscious experience, but before I do this I would like to stay where we are at the moment and see if there is another way of approaching these matters that leads us to the conclusion expressed above.

More on the human brain

In chapter 20 I left you with the fantasy of clasping the brain of a deceased person in your hands and thinking of how it was when it was a living entity, 'an organic whole, energised and buzzing with the activity of billions of minute nerve cells firing and communicating with each other across trillions of synapses by means of tiny biochemical changes'. I then asked you to think of all this as just *one* activity rather than lots of different activities, 'one object engaged in one activity'.

But now we are no longer considering the brain to be 'an object in itself'. We are thinking of it as part of a larger whole, ultimately the universe itself. How are we to argue in favour of this?

To begin with, for our brain to do anything at all it needs a constant supply of oxygen and other nutrients. These are provided by other organs of the body and conveyed to the brain by a network of blood vessels. Of course, when considering what underlies conscious awareness, our usual way of thinking—our subjective representation of the world—does not include the participation of the lungs, heart, liver, and so on; but there is no reason to suppose that Nature itself makes such a distinction. Consciousness requires a living body, and hence the body is a participant in the activity of consciousness. Indeed, each physical part of the body connects with several areas of the brain by bundles of nerve fibres. The activity in these fibres (and the areas of the brain to which they connect) is associated both with sensations and feeling and with the regulation of movement and functioning of these body parts.

What does a living body require? A complex, well-tuned environment such as exists on Earth—neither too hot nor too cold; with an atmosphere and magnetic field that each protects life from the dangerous rays of the Sun; with a plentiful supply of oxygen, water, and essential nutrients; with a history that allows evolution to proceed far enough for the emergence of intelligent life-forms. We may go further and consider what conditions need to be in place for all these requirements to emerge. And thus we continue.

We now find ourselves approaching the position where we can say that consciousness is an activity of the universe rather than any object in it, such as the human brain. But we can only do this when we relinquish ways of thinking that represent the world constructed by the mind—in fact, you may say, by the brain itself!

Now let's approach the same assertion, namely that we may consider any conscious event to be an activity of the universe itself, using the line of reasoning provided in Part V for objects and their activities generally.

A discrete conscious event as an activity of the universe
Up to now I have been considering the brain and conscious activity in general terms, but I have stressed numerous times the importance of applying this kind of analysis to any specified token event occurring in real space-time. Since we are discussing conscious activity, once more we find

ourselves having recourse to our, by now, familiar friend 'discrete conscious event'. Every DCE is an activity occurring at a unique location in space-time; normally we attribute this activity to the brain of the individual concerned, but can we think of any DCE as an activity of the universe?

Back in chapter 2 I listed the kinds of events that we may be conscious of. Broadly speaking, these are events in the external world, activities and processes occurring in our body, and activity originating in our brain. The discussion above applies to any of these and each may contribute, alone or in combination, to a DCE. For present purposes I shall consider a DCE that is occurring directly as a response to an event in our external world (as opposed to a thought, memory, dream, etc.) Such an experience requires the participation of one or more of our sensory systems—visual, auditory, olfactory, and so on—which, when our peripheral sensory organs (eyes, ears, nose, etc.) are stimulated, convey this information to our brain for further processing. Incidentally, especially these days, there is no reason why we should not include in this the participation of technology such as spectacles, hearing aids, telescopes, and microscopes. These devices dramatically enhance what we are able to perceive of our world, i.e. our conscious awareness of reality. What about pictures, television, videos, the internet etc. and, in the auditory modality, the telephone, radio, sound recordings, television again, etc.? Most definitely: whatever the medium is whereby we become conscious of an event originating in our external world (e.g. a distant galaxy whose image we see on our television set) the activity of that medium is part of that conscious event. We'll explore more of this later, but for the present, let's keep it simple!

Just at this moment I have a conscious representation of a blue cup on my desk that until some moments ago was full of tea that I brewed myself. How do we explain the occurrence of this unique DCE? Ordinarily, we would think of it as something the brain does and we would try to devise an explanation based on our knowledge of the brain's intricate physiological structure and functioning ('Account 1'). Let us instead consider, as we have previously done with examples of other events, activity *in addition to* that of my brain that is, of necessity, associated with the occurrence of this event ('Account 2'). Thus, unlike our normal way of construing the world (Account 1), we do not make any distinctions that entail the relative importance of any of these activities; nor do we consider only those that are most useful for normal purposes. We assume that Nature does likewise.

As well as how my brain processes the stimulation that it is receiving from my immediate environment, a necessary contribution to my DCE are photons of a certain wavelength, associated with the colour blue, coming from the cup, that impinge on the retinae of both my eyes. The receptors on my retinae, thus stimulated, send signals to my brain which are processed and provide me, in some way not currently understood, with the conscious experience of seeing a blue object which I identify as a cup, one of a certain size and shape, in a certain position, at a certain distance from me, and so on.

At this juncture it may pay to remind ourselves that my brain is not constructing a replica of what is objectively present, the 'something out there' in the real world that is responsible for this conscious experience. I might object to this statement and say, 'Well, it certainly looks like a cup to me!' but remember, nothing in the real world has the property 'looking like …' or 'having an appearance of'. 'What the world looks like' is, by definition, created by the mind of the observer.

Now let's proceed one step further and ask, 'Where do these photons of visible light originate?' The cup itself does not discharge them. One answer could be that they originate from the Sun and are streaming through a window in front of me. However, on this occasion they are emanating from electric light bulbs that are illuminating the room in which I am seated. Some of these photons are absorbed by the cup, and the ones of wavelength 'blue' are being re-emitted. So from the perspective of the real world we have to say that the light bulbs and their activity are part of the activity of my being consciously aware of my cup.

Now we take another step, one that again is moving us ever further away from Account 1, our usual way of thinking about these matters. I'll express it in the form of an assertion. Part of the activity of my being consciously aware of the cup is that which requires the cup to be in the particular place and time at which I perceive it. The activity in question was in fact undertaken by me about 30 minutes ago, when I went to the kitchen to make the cup of tea which I then brought to my desk; I drank the last mouthful of tea about 10 minutes ago and placed the cup *exactly* where I see it now.

It is essential, as ever, to keep in mind that I am now always referring to a DCE that actually happened. So, for example, I am not talking in general terms about the act of 'putting the empty cup back on my desk'; the actual conscious event that I am referring to involves the cup being in a certain position and orientation (e.g. with reference to the position of its handle). If I had placed it in a different position, I would be talking about a different DCE: something different ('X') must have happened for me to place the cup in a different position and something different again to account for why X happened, and so on. The same goes for the timing of the event, in the case of which we might consider all the circumstances that led to my looking at my cup *at that particular point in time* as opposed to any other.

Now, let's consider my activity 'making the cup of tea'. Amongst other things, I filled the kettle with water and put it on the heater; took a cup down from one of the hooks; opened the cupboard door where the tea is kept; and I think you can guess the rest! By the way, when I went to the fridge to get the milk I turned on the radio to catch the latest news, and while waiting for the tea to brew I fed the cats. Oh, I also had to answer door—the postman delivered a parcel. As far as I am concerned, and anybody observing me, the last three actions were not part of my activity making this cup of tea. But we have no reason to suppose that Nature itself distinguishes these events according to their salience for that particular activity. This carving up of the world as we experience it is what *we* observers do and it makes perfect sense[78] (and we'd be in a complete mess if we didn't do it). Moreover, change or eliminate any or all of these three events above and you change my DCE of the empty cup that we have been talking about; I will probably have a similar DCE but it will not be the same one at the same space-time locality.

Suppose now that another event that happens while I am making the tea is the phone ringing and the first thing I hear when I answer it is the voice of one of my friends asking me, 'What are you doing now?' I reply, 'I'm just making a cup of tea.' 'We thought you were coming to our meeting,' my friend responds. Oops! I completely forgot about this. 'It's OK,' my friend says, 'we're unlikely to get on to business that concerns you so you don't need to come.' I then finish making my tea.

Is it not the case that my friend's decision to excuse my attendance at the meeting is part of the activity of my conscious experience of the cup on my desk that I have been discussing? If she had not been so accommodating, I would have quickly turned off the kettle, gathered up what I needed, put on my coat, and left the house without making the tea. Hence: no conscious experience of the cup on my desk at all.

As with previous such analyses, we may continue by launching off into a series of discussions about how I came to be sitting at my desk at the moment of the DCE in question; how I came to acquire the cup in the first place; how both the cup and I came into existence; and so on. I

---

[78] Since observers are themselves part of the real world, it would be more correct to say, 'Nature only does this through the activity of the brains of sentient beings.'

suspect you will agree with me that by now, pursuing the argument at this level would be an unnecessary burden on your patience! I hope therefore you can see the rationale behind my assertion that this particular DCE, as with any DCE, is not 'an isolated event' but an activity that is part of an organic whole, the universe itself.

A slight diversion

Was I correct when I told my friend, in the above scenario, that I was making a cup of tea? 'Of course you were!' you reply. If I decided to attend the meeting and I told my colleagues when I arrived that I was making a cup of tea when my friend phoned, would I be telling the truth? 'Of course you would!' you reply. But if you are correct both times, where's the cup of tea that I was making? And especially, as in the second scenario, if no cup of tea were produced, how could I have been making a cup of tea?

We could have a long and meaningful discussion about this (and I am sure philosophers do) but we are only teased by such questions when we are talking about how we represent and communicate about the world our mind constructs: they have no meaning when asked of the objective world, which we have no reason to suppose identifies any ongoing activity with reference to its intended outcome, whether realised or not.

Internal representations

I have been talking about awareness of my external world, but does anything about what I have been arguing apply to awareness of my *internal* world, such as thoughts, images, memories and dreams? Recall that these are all activities involving the brain and are not 'things', and they may occur independent of any immediate input from the external world—for instance my visualising a blue cup without one being present. The answer is yes; any of these experiences occur within the context of a wider range of activity, internal and external, both ongoing and past (e.g. my imagining a blue cup is based on previous activity involving cups and the colour blue in the external world).

The ocean metaphor again

It may be helpful now to remind you of the image of a huge ocean, as described in chapter 25, as an analogy of the universe. As with anything that our mind identifies as 'an event', we can envisage occurrences of DCEs as areas of activity of this universe, recurring patterns in the way its material is arranged and behaves. According to the conclusions drawn in this chapter, it seems more apposite to imagine each DCE as a diffuse patch of brightness as opposed to just one bright dot representing a Host such as a human brain.

As it stands, however, this is a snapshot image at a fixed moment in time and does not capture the ever-changing nature of the universe, the constant toing and froing of matter and activity. We can add motion to this image if we choose, but let's instead introduce what we have concluded about time and existence in Part IV. Now we try to conceive all events in this ocean as occurring in space-time over the whole history of the universe, including those 'bright patches' representing those locations where it engages in the activity of being consciously aware of its own structure and activity. And all these bright spots of activity exist: none can be said to only exist in the *universe's* past, present or future.

Meditation on an unusual way of thinking

Each one of us is a part of the universe and everything any of us does, says or thinks is an activity of the universe. This is very much the opposite of how we understand ourselves and our everyday life. So how about spending some time thinking about yourself from this perspective and what you are doing? In Appendix IV I provide some of my own musings which I refer to as 'Some digressionary consequences'.

Meditation on 'the universal Host'

Almost at the start of our journey, in my discussion about human consciousness, I made the tripartite distinction Host [You], Person [You] and Soul [You], with Host [You] being your material body, engaged in 'doing' Person [You], including conscious activity and awareness of being (i.e. Soul [You]). Now I am saying that everything Host [You] does is an activity of the universe. Hence, it seems as though there is only one Host, the material universe, and everything that we refer to as 'consciousness' is the universe being aware of itself and its own activity—'a universal Host' with 'a universal Soul' maybe?

Does this bring us any closer to our destination? Does it smack too much of mysticism or religion? Or is it a reasonable conclusion based on rational arguments and an objective perspective of the world, consistent, at least, with current scientific knowledge? I invite you to consider these questions before embarking on the next stage of our journey.

CHAPTER 27

THE UNIVERSAL SOUL

We are now coming close to providing answers to all the questions posed at the start of our journey. Let us therefore draw together our conclusions and present a comprehensive, standalone account of the Theory of the Soul.

1. The theory adopts a position of **indirect** or **representational realism**. The universe exists independently of observers such as human beings, although any observer must be part of the universe. However, our perception, knowledge and understanding of the world can only be based on what our minds are capable of consciously creating from the limited information received by our senses. Our representation of reality is not a true replication; it is more like a map rather than the territory that a map represents.

2. The theory is not a *scientific* one as it is not amenable to testing or disproof. However, it is **materialistic** and adopts a moderately **scientistic** perspective: by the application of logic and rational thought along with the scientific method we can gain a more accurate representation of reality, even though this is still only akin to a map.

3. The theory is **atheistic**: there is no internal or external observer of the universe, such as a deity, a creator, or an intelligent designer.

4. When considering an individual human being ('X'— meaning you, me, the name of the individual, etc.) the theory adopts a working model that distinguishes Host [X] (the material body, in particular the brain and nervous system, of that individual) and Person [X] (the unique identity of that individual). Thus Person [X] is not a being or entity, but the activity of Host [X]. The activity of a Host that is of central importance here is consciousness, implying that what we term 'the mind' is something the Host does.

5. One further distinction is that of Soul [X]. This refers to X's 'awareness of self' or 'awareness of being': aware of being the person they are, aware that *they* are experiencing what is experienced, likewise feeling what is felt, thinking what is thought, and so on. Thus 'Host' may be defined more broadly as any object that is capable of consciousness, including awareness of self.

6. As 'awareness of self', an individual's Soul includes awareness of always having been 'the same person' in the past, and the anticipation of always being that person in the future, despite continuous changes in the Host's material composition, structure and functioning. However, the theory itself does not accept the assumption of preservation of personal identity from moment to moment *in reality*.

7. The theory is based on a **space-time** representation of the universe throughout its entire existence, from its inception to its (hypothetical) demise. Every event (loosely speaking, matter behaving in a certain way) occurs at its own unique location in four-dimensional space-time.

8. Putting together 6 and 7, the theory adopts a construct termed 'discrete conscious event' (DCE). A DCE is any moment of conscious activity by a Host. Like any other event, each DCE occurs at a unique location in space-time. The constructs Person and Soul may still be applied.

9. The theory adheres to the doctrine of **eternalism** (the 'B-Theory of time', or at least a version of it). Time is real, but how we experience it does not duplicate its nature in reality. Past, present and future may *only* be defined by reference to an actual event or moment in time, i.e. what happens before, simultaneous with, or after that reference point. Hence there is no *absolute* past, present and future that defines what exists (now), what no longer exists, and what has yet to exist in the universe. In reality, every event in the universe's history 'exists'.

10. The above applies to an event defined as a DCE. Hence consciousness, time and existence are inextricably linked. A DCE defines 'now' (what *exists* now in the universe), what no longer exists (is in the universe's past), and what has yet to exist (is in the universe's future) *for that Host only*. It follows from 9 that all DCEs throughout the universe's entire history exist.

11. The Host of any DCE is structured to be aware of a past and of the present; it is also structured in a way that largely determines the DCE in the immediate future. Thus, throughout the lifetime of individual X, X experiences a seamless stream of conscious events (interrupted by periods of unconsciousness) along a timeline from past to present to future. Hence the impression of continuity of personal identity over time, despite continuous changes in the material composition, structure and functioning of the Hosts of each DCE that extend over X's lifetime.

12. The theory adopts a **holistic** or **organistic** representation of the universe (though not in any mystical sense, and still strictly **deterministic**). That is, it is conceived as one organic whole, all parts of which are inter-related in lawful ways. Every event is an activity of the universe itself.

13. From 12 we may say that the composition of the universe is such that at certain locations in space and time it is consciously aware of its own structure and activity; this includes awareness of being aware of such.

211

14. The universe's self-awareness is experienced at the level of each individual Host in space-time. The experience of awareness of being more than one Host is not physically possible. More precisely, we can make these statements with reference to each individual DCE rather than Host. In everyday parlance. we would simply say that we can only have the conscious experiences of one person, the person we are identifying as 'I' or 'me'.

15. From 12 and 13, you and everyone else who lived before you, who lives at the same time as you, and who will live after you, may be said to share the same awareness of being or Soul; we may call this the Universal Soul.

Meditation

You and I and everybody else may be said to share the same awareness of being or Soul; we may call this the Universal Soul.

In the next chapter we shall examine all the questions I raised at the beginning of this book and answer them unequivocally. But before that, I invite you to look again at some of those questions and to consider what answers emerge from our explorations.

You may also like to think ahead about the consequences that emerge from these answers for you personally. Are they exciting, comforting, frightening, depressing, or a mixture of all of these?

CHAPTER 28

OUR QUESTIONS ANSWERED

Let us without further ado proceed to answer all the questions we asked at the beginning of this book, based on where our deliberations have led us.

Why was I born the person I am? Why wasn't I born somebody else?

The 'I' above refers to the questioner's awareness of being. Now consider our conclusion expressed in point 15 of the previous chapter:

You and everyone else who lived before you, who lives at the same time as you, and who will live after you, may be said to share the same awareness of being or Soul.

So the 'I' that is aware of being you in the above two questions is the 'I' that is aware of being any and every other person in time and space (from points 9 and 10). You may say. 'I am everyone.'[79] But this 'I' can only experience being

---

[79] It is difficult to find the language to express these assertions unambiguously, perhaps because they are so illogical to the way we experience the world.

each person individually. And that experience is always one of having been that individual and continuing to be that individual in the future until death.

What happens to me when I die? What happens to my soul when I die? Does my soul live on?

When Host [You] stops functioning, it is no longer capable of being (or 'doing') Person [You]. In other words, in no meaningful sense can you continue being the person you are now once you have died. However, our adherence to the doctrine of eternalism (point 9) allows us to say that all you did and experienced between your birth and your death still exists in space-time.

What is not affected by death is Soul [You], your awareness of being some entity that can function as a Host (for present purposes a human being). Once again:

You and I and everybody else may be said to share the same awareness of being or Soul.

Figuratively speaking (it is difficult to express this otherwise) we are always aware of being someone (i.e. 'a Host', or we could say 'the Host of a DCE') in the manner described in point 14. So what does happen to me when I die? Here, we must be very careful with our words: when the person I am does not exist (e.g. after my death or before my birth) I am still consciously aware of being some person. Again, strictly speaking we should say 'some Host' and this could be any Host in the universe, there being no reason to restrict this to planet Earth.

Now, this statement is open to a good deal of misinterpretation, and to avoid this requires us to think more precisely about the implications of the theory summarised in the last chapter. We can start this off by emphasising that the statement is not equivalent to the popular notion of transmigration of souls, namely that when we die we are reincarnated as another person (and that we have previous lived as another person). Critical scrutiny reveals the evidence presented in its favour is seriously flawed, and earlier in our journey I rejected the idea on rational and logical grounds. So why is our present position so different from this? To understand why this is so, it is necessary:

(i) to consider this question, not at the level of what we perceive as the individual person (a Host's unique identity [e.g. John Smith] that is continuous over time from birth to death), but in terms of individual DCEs occurring in their unique space-time locations (point 8); and

(ii) to adhere to the doctrine that, from a universal perspective, all events, including DCEs, exist (9 and 10).

Now consider the traditional idea of reincarnation in its most simplistic, not to say facile, terms. A person whom we shall call M has her last moment of consciousness (her last DCE) on May 21st, dies and ceases to be. Sometime later her soul migrates to a newly born child, N and at a certain time N has his first DCE. When N dies a similar event happens: the soul now migrates to another future individual, whom we may call 'O'. Thus migration of the soul proceeds over a consecutive series of lives along a fixed timeline, from the past (the lives I have lived), to the present (the life I live now), to the future (the lives I have yet to live).

Although the theory of Universal Awareness is based on the concept of a Universal Soul—the universe is consciously aware of itself and its own activity—it does *not* predict that we each live a succession of different lives along a fixed timeline in the manner described. Our everyday understanding of the world compels us to think of the survival of the soul in this manner, but we must try to set this aside and see things from the radically different perspective adopted by the theory, which is by no means easy.

Of all the countless DCEs that exist in the universe, no special distinction is given to those we think of as the first and the last in the life of any person, unlike the usual idea of transmigration of the soul described above. To understand this, first recall the meditation discussed in chapters 3 and 4 in which you imagined becoming your friend and *vice versa* (in effect, swapping souls). If this were possible, the first DCE you would experience as your friend would include having been that person as far back as you can remember (previous DCEs). The same applies to the replicated Host in our thought experiments about teleportation.

Now let's remind ourselves that all DCEs exist in space-time. There is no absolute sense in which some exist now, some existed in the past, and some will exist in the future; they do so only from the perspective of an individual DCE. So when, say, I have 'my last DCE' and die, my timeline— what is my past, present and future—ceases. It makes no sense to ask what happens to me when I die, from the standpoint of my soul: the Universal Soul is timeless in this respect. But it is very difficult not ask oneself this question. The best we can do for an answer is to say, 'When I die I become aware of being someone else—another Host' but the everyday assumptions underlying this way of speaking are not part of the theory of Universal Awareness.

What happens to the people I know when they die? Do their souls live on somewhere? Shall my soul ever meet their soul again?

The answers to these questions should by now be self-evident. At death, a person ceases to be. 'Spirits of the departed' and their contacting us do not feature in our answers, neither do Heaven and Hell. However, our conclusions do have far-reaching implications for our understanding of death and how we are to grieve.

Can my soul live on in the form of another person, so that after I die I am born again—reincarnated—as another individual? Indeed, have I lived as someone else before being the person I am now?'

These questions are answered above.

If I never experienced self-awareness before I was born, and will never again experience it after I have died, does this mean I have only one chance of living as a conscious, self-aware being, namely the individual I am now? If that is so, then what is it that decided that I would be the individual I am and not some other person?

The answer to the first questions is clearly no and the second conundrum does not arise with Universal Awareness.

Is it the case that if I only have this one chance of experiencing being a person (or any sentient being) I would have lost that chance if the person I am had never been born?

Again the answer is no.

Can the soul live on as some form of awareness, but not awareness of being any *thing*, any individual?

No. The experience of the Soul is always associated with a Host.

Or is death oblivion, as when we are rendered unconscious, but without any return to consciousness?

No. In fact this is a good moment to note something important that you may have already realised. Universal Awareness, it seems, is eternal. Whilst it is likely that sentient beings can only thrive in the universe within a window of space-time, outside of which no life is possible, there is no beginning or end to Universal Awareness. This seems rather bizarre but remember that our awareness of being does not proceed along a continuous, fixed universal timeline, such that it all started one day and it is moving along relentlessly until the day it ends. There is no escape; we are forever destined to be aware.

We can now see how the theory of the Universal Soul provides answers to all these profound questions. However, our everyday notions of time and existence make it very difficult for each one of us to understand how we can all share the same Soul, as we are conceiving it, with every other Host in our universe, when it appears to us that we are only ever aware of being the same person throughout our lives.

More answers

Let us now turn our attention to the various thought experiments and conundrums that we encountered on our travels. The first one is the exercise introduced in chapter 3 in which you imagine that you switch identities with someone for a minute and then switch back. How would you know if you had or had not succeeded and how would they know? The answer appears to be that in either case there is no way of knowing, because nothing would have changed. Clearly this is consistent with the concept of a shared Soul. 'Being aware of being you' and 'being aware of being your friend' at any time are activities of the universe, but are experienced separately, not simultaneously. This gives the illusion of 'separate Souls', but there is really only one Soul.

In chapters 6 and 7 I invited you to consider all the possible events and conditions that need to have occurred or been in place for you to have been born at all and thus have the experience of 'awareness of being'. We can now see that the idea of a Universal Soul means, in a manner of speaking, that you are always 'aware of being'; it is not something that depends on the precise combination of a myriad of circumstances, as would be the case if your 'awareness of being' died with you.

From chapters 8 to 13 we wrestled with the problem of personal identity and the preservation of the Soul despite the fact that our physical constitution (Host)—the material of which we are made and how it is structured and functions— is continuously changing, on occasions drastically so, over time. Also recall our thought experiments about replicating a particular individual in the teleportation scenario; the problem about the two identical Hosts 'having different Souls' seemed to cause us lots of confusion. Now we can see that there is no paradox or problem at all in any of this.

Consequences

Clearly, if we accept the idea of a Universal Soul, then there are profound consequences for how we understand our humanity—for example the moral basis for our behaviour, how we should treat one another, how we come to terms with death (ours and that of loved ones); and how we view religion. In the next chapter I shall provide you with some of my thoughts on these matters; but first I invite you think about them for yourself.

CHAPTER 29

PANDORA'S BOX

We are all one. You and I share the same Soul. I am you, and you are me. And we share this Soul with everyone else.

If you think only of human life on Earth, then you are everyone who lives, who has lived, and who will live. All the experiences that anybody has ever had and will have are your experiences. More than that: you are experiencing them now. But you can only be aware of being just one of these people at any one moment—'the person you are now'—and his or her history, his or her future. When you are 'not that person' you do not cease to be aware; your Soul does not end. You are 'someone else'.

You are everyone around you, and they are you. You are all those people whom you have admired or would admire if you knew them; everyone you have envied; everyone you have wanted to be.

All the moments of joy and excitement that anyone experiences in this world are experienced by you. The lover's passion, the parents' delight at their first child, the victor's triumph, and the ordinary, everyday feelings of pleasure that being alive brings.

It must also be that every unhappiness, every anxiety, and every disappointment in the world is being experienced by you. Right now. The anguish of the jilted lover; the grief of the bereaved spouse; the fear of the bullied child; the sadness of the lonely old person; the everyday worries and upsets that beset everyone.

And so it must also be true that you are everyone you have *never* wanted to be, everyone you have hated, despised, and pitied: the fool, the drunkard, the pauper, the villain, the insane, the wretched, the sick, and the dying. All their experiences are your experiences. Every pain they experience is your pain; every sorrow your sorrow; every terror your terror. All the tears of the world are your tears. You are the pitiful child who is sick and starving. You are that child's mother, driven to despair. You are the old woman, demented and abandoned. You are the injured soldier, dying in agony on the battlefield far from home. Whatever they are feeling, you are feeling. But at any one time you can only be aware of the feelings of one person, 'the person you are now'.

All the joy in the world is your joy; all the suffering is your suffering. What is more, you reap the rewards of all the good that you do. Every pleasure you give to others is your pleasure. Every hope, your hope. Every comfort, your comfort. Each kindness you give, you receive. The sacrifices you make for others are for yourself.

And equally, every unkindness you do is unkindness to yourself. The hurt you cause others is your hurt, the fear your fear. You are the bully and the one you are bullying, the torturer and the one you are torturing, the liar and the one you are deceiving, the tyrant and the one who is cringing in fear of you, the slave owner and his wretched slave. You are the husband who cheats on his wife and the wife herself. The beggar you ignore in the street is you. You are the camp guard whipping that poor emaciated creature. Enjoying yourself? You are that human skeleton, suffering with every lash their fear, agony, and despair. And you are each of the millions of others who were victim to those extremes of inhumanity all too recent in our present. Everything they suffer, you suffer.

And so it must be that Your Soul is Our Soul, universal, eternal and always. For in reality, there is no distinction *you* and *everybody else*. There is only *we* and *us*. We are always somebody, and somebody is always we, with no beginning or end: all is timeless.

I have only been speaking of human beings. What about animals? Maybe they, or some of them, have some form of self-awareness. And if so, then it is *our* awareness; we are every such creature that has ever lived, is living, and shall live.

And this is just on the planet Earth. Maybe—most certainly, some people would say—there are beings on planets across the vast expanse of the universe that are also capable of self-awareness. What sort of lives do they lead? Whatever the answer, *their* experiences are *our* experiences.

If you accept all of this as possible, likely, or true, is there anything we can do about it? It seems from all our deliberations that everything in our universe—its composition, structure and activity at any time—is predetermined, and there is nothing we can do to alter it: there is no escape. There is no heaven waiting for us. No resting in peace. No welcome oblivion. There is only eternal life and awareness.

But is there hope?
I have painted a bleak picture. But the proverbial glass is both half-empty and half-full. We can comfort ourselves knowing that 'the good old times' are still happening, and we are still enjoying them. All the loved ones whom we have left behind and whom we miss so dearly are still leading the lives they had with us. All the pleasures that they had, they are still having. Nothing and no one really dies. And all their pleasures are our pleasures too.

And yet…perhaps the prospect that I set out in the last chapter is not so different from that which faces any person, you and me included, in his or her life. You (I hope) and I may be contented with our lot at the moment, but who is to say that horrific, life-changing misfortunes are not in store for one or both of us tomorrow, next week, or in the years to come? And if we knew that such were to be the case, would we still be thinking now, 'I have, and have had, a life worth living'?

And if we feel that our life isn't worth living, if we are indeed suffering from illness, poverty, misery, or the cruelty of others, we can think that we are also enjoying the life of someone more fortunate. In fact, we are many, indeed all, such fortunate people. We cannot, while we are experiencing being the individual we are, also experience being such a person. Many people, whatever kind of life they are leading, may relish the idea that death is not oblivion, and that their experience of living is perpetual.

Moral implications

What are the moral implications of the Universal Soul? It seems to me that there is an obvious and simple consequence for how we are to behave towards one another, one that has already served us well for centuries. This is the Golden Rule: 'Do unto others as you would have them do unto you.' There is also the Silver Rule: 'Do not do unto others as you would not have them do unto you.' Nothing is ever quite that simple, of course, but from our point of view the basis of these rules is clear: 'Whatever you do unto others you do also unto yourself.' This appears to render the rule somewhat less altruistic, but perhaps provides a stronger incentive to apply it than the vague promise of heavenly reward in an afterlife.

PART VII

FURTHER EXPLORATIONS OF
UNIVERSAL AWARENESS

CHAPTER 30

THOUGHTS ON THE MEANING OF 'UNIVERSAL AWARENESS'

The concept of universal awareness, along with that of universal soul, is in principle a simple one: awareness, including awareness of being aware, is a natural property of the universe, something *the universe does* that is manifested at rare space-time locations where its structure makes this possible. It does not depend on any paranormal claims or the invention of any supernatural entity or force or energy unknown to science. It is entirely materialistic. However, it does become a much more ambitious theory when it is used to address profound questions such as 'Why was I born the person I am?' and 'What happens to me when I die?' Having relied on the theory to fulfil these explicit aims, I do not think it is satisfactory simply to put it to bed and only spend our time contemplating these answers and their implications. Indeed, matters such as these are only part of a wider picture that emerges from this way of thinking about our universe. So let's press on and see where this way of thinking may lead us. Incidentally, if you are not convinced by the idea of universal awareness please note my use of the phrase 'way of thinking'; *all* our ways of thinking about the universe, even those offered by scientists, are not reality itself but our mind's way of representing reality, with all the limitations that this implies.

Awareness on a spectrum

I think a useful starting point for further exploration is for us to contemplate once again the metaphorical image of our universe as one vast ocean of activity in which those rare regions where conscious activity occurs are represented by diffuse patches of brightness. Now, when *I* do this, one question that comes to mind is whether awareness[80], rather than being an all-or-none property that occurs or does not occur in a particular part of the universe, may be better represented as having the property of a spectrum or continuum that extends over the entire universe, including inanimate as well as living matter. Thus, in our oceanic representation, rather than 'patches of brightness', we imagine shades of grey, from very dark to very bright. If so, in what terms are we to conceive of this 'universal spectrum of awareness'?

There may be several possibilities and I am offering you just one for your consideration. For this purpose, it will be easier now to temporarily put aside our oceanic metaphor whereby we speak of 'parts' of one organic whole rather than separate entities, and revert to the latter, everyday way of thinking though now and again it may pay us to consider how our ideas may be represented by the aforesaid metaphor.) In fact we have touched upon this question in earlier chapters (e.g. chapter 2) when I have talked about how we experience different levels of consciousness, whether creatures other than humans have the capability of being conscious in some

---

[80] If you find yourself becoming confused about my varying use of the terms 'awareness', 'consciousness', etc. it may help you to revisit my remarks on this subject in chapter 2.

less advanced way, and if it is possible for humans to build machines that have some degree of consciousness. (There is also much discussion by scientists about how consciousness develops in very young babies.) But what is proposed above is clearly something much more ambitious than this, what I have called 'a universal spectrum of awareness'. For example, with respect to living things, we would normally exclude any non-animal species from our list of organisms that we would classify as being capable of consciousness. Even so, an internet search will reveal to you that there are a few biologists who are prepared to consider that if we broaden our definition of consciousness, plants can be thought of as being conscious (i.e. as 'sentient beings'), though in a more basic sense than animals.

Could this spectrum of awareness extend to non-living objects? Surely not, unless we are asking the question about human-made machines. But let's think about this further. To keep it simple, we'll just consider the case where we assert that 'X is aware of Y' where Y is an object external to X What do we mean when we say this?

Meditation
The question to consider in this meditation is whether it is meaningful in some way to say that two *inanimate* objects are 'aware of each other' and whether this has any connection with our everyday understanding of 'being aware'. You may choose any two objects you like, say the Sun and the Earth. In what way can they be said to be aware of one another? (In the chapter to follow I shall return to the example of a cup of tea and the table on which it is resting, so you may choose this one instead.)

CHAPTER 31

A UNIVERSAL SPECTRUM OF AWARENESS?

Panpsychism
In recent times there has been an upsurge of interest, not just amongst philosophers but also a minority of scientists, in a doctrine with an ancient lineage called 'panpsychism'. Simply put, panpsychism asserts that whereas it is generally considered that 'having a mind' is something that applies only to sentient beings such as humans and possibly other species, there are ways of thinking that allow to accredit mind-like properties not only to more basic forms of life, such as plants and unicellular organisms, but even to inanimate objects including, some would propose, entities as small as subatomic particles.

Of course, serious advocates of panpsychism do not believe that such objects are conscious and have an inner life as humans do. Rather, it is considered that mind-like properties are universal, but they only achieve their most advanced level of sophistication, so far as we know, in an organ with the complexity of the functioning human brain.[81]

Panpsychism is a highly controversial proposition and I am not relying on any existing version of it here. However the discussion that follows has some of the flavour of panpsychism. It is intended only as *one possible answer* to the question whether it is valid and useful to think of a universal continuum of awareness. There may be better answers, and indeed you may prefer to devise your own—it is not essential that you accept my account to progress to the other topics addressed in this section. But it is non-controversial and is not based on any strong assumptions that have to be taken in good faith.

Awareness at its most basic

So let's consider the meditation in the previous chapter: is it meaningful in some way to say that two *inanimate* objects are 'aware of each other'? I'll first address this question using my example of the cup of tea in chapter 26, except that this time it is in front of *you*.

As a preliminary, let's revisit the question 'What does it mean to say that *you* are aware of the cup of tea?' Well, largely it's that you see it with your eyes, meaning that the cup is reflecting photons of light from whatever is illuminating the environment (the Sun or an electrical source) and some of these are stimulating receptors on the retinae of your eyes which then send signals to a structure in your brain called the thalamus, and on to your visual cortex for further processing. There are of course other modalities through which you can

---

[81] Hence panpsychism is not an appeal for animistic ways of thinking, whereby we endow non-sentient objects with human characteristics such as thoughts and emotions. I am sure I am not unique in the irrational remorse I sometimes feel when throwing out an old jacket or a piece of furniture that has served me well over the years. Also, like many people I experience great empathy for a tree that is about to be chopped down.

be aware of the cup and its contents: you may feel it with your hand, and both smell and taste its contents. So, for example, there are receptors on or near the periphery of your body (your skin, nose and tongue) that are stimulated when you touch or come near to the cup and its contents, and signals from these receptors are conveyed to the relevant parts of your brain. Thus we can say that at the most basic level, your being aware of the cup of tea means that this object is having effects on you that would not occur if it were not present.

If we consider 'awareness' at this basic, mechanistic level then we may say that the cup of tea is also aware of you, since *you* are having effects on *it* that would not occur if you were not present. Obviously, the effects in question are much slighter and more subtle than the effects that the object is having on you by virtue of the fact that you have a sensory system that responds to a far wider range of stimulation than does the object—we might say there is 'asymmetry of awareness'. But remember we are thinking of 'awareness' at its most primitive level. We shall see what the effects of you on the cup of tea are when we now move on to consider the case where *both* objects are inanimate.

For two inanimate objects, let's choose the cup of tea again and the table on which it rests. In line with the above reasoning, we may say these two objects are aware of each other by, for one thing, photons being reflected from the cup onto the table and *vice versa*. (Although you as the observer play no part in this, you may see some reflection of the cup on the table and likewise, perhaps, of the table on the exterior surface of the cup.) The cup will also cast a shadow on the table, meaning that there is less light reaching the table at that particular location than at others. There will be a mutual gravitational attraction between the two objects, albeit very weak. There will also be a strong repulsive electromagnetic force between the cup and the table, preventing the former from sinking through the latter owing to the Earth's gravity.

When there is tea in the cup, some of the heat will be transferred from the cup to the table; that is, the molecules of which the table is composed will be in a more agitated state under and around the base of the cup.

Suppose that you drink the tea and, being a very tidy person, you immediately take your empty cup to the kitchen to be washed. Now the area of the table on which the cup was resting will retain some of the heat transferred from the cup, although this effect (the extra agitation of the molecules) will not take long to fade. Again at its most basic, we can say that the table retains a short-term memory of its awareness of the cup of tea. This accords with the doctrine espoused in chapter 6 that memory is an activity (hence, say, a permanent ring left by your cup on the tabletop is not such a good example, though maybe we can equate this with the table's long-term memory of your cup of tea).

Now, in the scenario I have described, it is not simply the case that the cup of tea is only 'aware' of the table and *vice versa*. Each will be 'aware' of the presence of many things in their environment in the kind of primitive ways I have described. For example, the cup of tea presently on *my* desk is aware, just at this moment, of a heavy lorry passing my house: it is vibrating very slightly. As with you and the cup of tea, there is what I have called 'asymmetrical awareness' in the relationship between these two objects: I doubt if the lorry is much affected by the teacup as it is passing by!

We can spend a lot of time performing the same exercise with different pairs of objects. In the previous chapter I suggested the Sun and the Earth. In what respects could we say the Earth is aware of the Sun? Well, again photons of light from the Sun are reaching the Earth's surface (and clouds in the Earth's atmosphere), likewise heat radiated from the Sun. Charged particles emitted by the Sun reach the Earth's atmosphere and from their collision with atoms there they release photons which strike the Earth's surface (the phenomenon of *aurora borealis*). The Earth is also significantly affected by the presence of the Sun's mass through gravitational attraction. We could go on to talk about the more far-reaching effects of the Sun's light, heat and mass on the Earth, but let's keep it simple and, in a manner similar to the above, consider the question 'Is the Sun aware of the Earth?' Again, at the most basic level we think of how the Sun is affected by the Earth and one way is that a minute proportion of its photons are reflected by the Earth and make their way back to the Sun. Not a huge effect, but an effect nonetheless. And as above, the Earth's mass significantly affects the Sun's motion through their mutual gravitational attraction.

Now all of this seems a long way from what we normally understand by 'consciousness' when are referring to human experience. For one thing, our conscious brain engages in the activity of creating a representation of its environment internally in a form that we experience as sensations, perceptions, feelings and emotions. Moreover, it constructs representations of its environment in the absence of the latter—by thinking, imagining, remembering, dreaming, and so on. But could it be that we can represent awareness as a continuum ranging from the most fundamental type, illustrated above[82], to the most complex, namely human consciousness? If so, what comes between these extremes? I invite you to pause and think about this before reading on.

---0---

What comes to my mind in answer to the above question are firstly various forms of life, and secondly machines made by humans. The only examples of both of these that we currently know of are those we find on planet Earth. Such

---

[82] To illustrate the points raised I have chosen everyday objects, but the same reasoning may be applied to microscopic entities such as individual molecules, atoms and even subatomic particles.

objects are structurally complex, increasingly so for living things as we ascend the phylogenetic scale, and likewise, by analogy, for machines. That is, they are increasingly sensitive and responsive to their environments and what they do with the stimulation that affects them. For example, a leaf on a plant responds to light from the Sun, and carbon dioxide and water in the atmosphere and soil, to create oxygen and glucose (photosynthesis).

Keep in mind that I am exploring the idea that an object can be said to be aware of other objects in its environment if it is affected by them. Thus, awareness is an interaction between objects, although, as stated earlier, it may be asymmetrical (as in the earlier example of yourself and the cup of tea) and need not be reciprocal (as with the lorry and the cup of tea).

Interactions between *living* things and their environment, such as photosynthesis, commonly produce long-lasting effects on the organism. For instance, all animal species learn from the results of their interactions with their environment. As noted above, some retain images, memories and dreams based on these interactions, of which they are able to display awareness independent of their immediate environment. They are thus said to 'possess an inner life' and at this level, 'consciousness' seems a more apposite term to use than mere 'awareness'. Related to this, *they may be aware of themselves being aware* (of whatever it is at the moment, including internal experiences): they have a sense of self and individuality; they are *conscious* of their environment and of themselves.[83]

---

[83] Consider once more the cup on the table. The cup is now empty and it has an interior shadow caused by the blocking of light by part of the cup facing the main light source. That is, photons of light that would otherwise impinge on the interior part of the cup are deflected by the intervening part. Perhaps the reasoning adopted here allows us to say that *at the most basic level* the cup is aware of itself and its own activity.

It is uncertain which animals have these capabilities, but humans certainly do and we have already considered that they may well be present in some intelligent species but less developed. Perhaps there are intelligent beings in the universe for whom these capabilities are even more highly developed than here on Earth. Hence, if we consider awareness to be on a spectrum of complexity, then at the lower end we have the example of a simple inanimate object being affected by another in the most basic ways, while at the upper end we have the most complex known form of awareness, namely human consciousness, whereby the sensory apparatus and brain respond in a highly sensitive manner to a wide range of physical stimulation emanating from the surrounding world; in humans at least, this includes awareness of self. In between these extremes we have species other than animals, and below them the biochemical precursors of the earliest life forms.

From this we may say that **'awareness is a universal property of matter'**. Over almost the entire universe it is only present at the most basic level I have described—the interactions between matter that occur 'according to the laws of Nature'. However, at rare and minute spacetime locations matter becomes more complex[84] in its composition and interaction with other matter; thus higher forms of 'awareness' emerge. These locations are found mainly on what we call planets (made up of matter in elemental and, more often, molecular form) that orbit stars (comprising matter, mostly in the form of the simplest elements, hydrogen and helium). So far, we know of only our planet on which these higher forms of awareness exist.

---

[84] In support of my arguments I am relying heavily on the term 'complex'. I apologise for the vagueness of this descriptor here, as it is clearly of central significance and a more precise definition of the term would be essential for a detailed exposition of the thesis being presented.

It may seem to you that this conclusion is not much more than a tame version of panpsychism (although it may not be supported by those who object to such a mechanistic and reductionist understanding of consciousness). As I have expressed it, it is still very much grounded in our way of representing the world as divided into separate objects (a cup of tea, a table, a lorry, etc.) each engaged in its own activities and causally influencing other objects. In fact, this has been a criticism of panpsychism itself. Clearly we need to consider this idea of a universal spectrum of awareness by reverting to our representation of the universe as one organic whole, as with our oceanic metaphor.

CHAPTER 32

SIGNIFICANT PROPERTIES OF UNIVERSAL AWARENESS

According to the very loose definition suggested in the previous chapter, 'awareness' is a ubiquitous property of the universe and is distributed along a spectrum, ranging from the basic physical means whereby 'matter affects other matter'—let's allow ourselves the use of the biological term 'environmental sensitivity' for this—to the highest level of consciousness that we know of. Personally I find the idea of a spectrum of awareness permeating the material universe compelling and it will make sense when considering the ideas that I shall now be presenting. But it is not *essential* to the validity of these ideas, so it's OK if you are unable to accept it. Or maybe you accept the idea of a spectrum of awareness that applies to all matter, but not on the basis that I have outlined. In that case, you may still find the modified version of our oceanic metaphor useful, i.e. levels of complexity of awareness represented by shades of grey in space-time.

It seems that awareness, *as conceived here*, accelerates up this spectrum at those locations where material becomes so complex (that term again) as to eventually enable, in some way not yet fully determined, the emergence of life. From thereon, over billions of years, life forms become more elaborate, and the capability of awareness exhibited by living material increases accordingly. Of course, 'awareness' in the sense of consciousness is not regarded as a defining property of life; environmental sensitivity is, and this is more akin to how I am using the term. Other properties of living organisms are their highly ordered structure and functioning, growth and development; internal regulation; and the ability to replicate. Each of these properties can be said to exist at basic levels in non-living, prebiotic forms.[85]

As far as we know, the locations of conscious activity as we normally understand it, are *only* those where life (again an activity of the universe) exists. That is, life is an essential but not sufficient condition: we generally assumed that we may have life without consciousness but not *vice versa*.[86]

The direction we shall now take is to examine more thoroughly the nature of conscious awareness as viewed from this universal and spectral standpoint. In doing so I shall discuss several properties of universal consciousness that can be seen to emerge and develop over time. Obviously, I can only do this with reference to intelligent life on Earth, but I think it is reasonable to suggest that my discussion may generalise to other intelligent life that may exist in the universe. These properties may be summarised, in a highly figurative manner, as follows:

Where the universe is conscious:

1. It tends to become **increasingly** so over time (think of those bright patches becoming even brighter)

---

[85] See Greene (2020) for a discussion of this.

[86] One day we may have machines capable of consciousness (though not having life as we understand it); but these can only be created by conscious beings. I shall be discussing matters such as this in due course.

2. It behaves in ways that **preserve** its consciousness (think of those bright patches persisting over time)

3. It behaves in ways that spatially **extend** its self-consciousness (think of those bright patches expanding over space in time).

In the chapters to follow, I shall illustrate what I mean by each of these properties. For the moment, if you're unsure about them, it might help you to consider that we can say something very similar about living matter on our planet.

CHAPTER 33

UNIVERSAL AWARENESS INCREASES OVER TIME

There are significant areas of human conscious activity that we might profitably examine from the standpoint that they are natural activities of the universe. One that has assumed great importance in the daily lives of human beings on Earth is the activity we call science.

Science: the acquisition and application of knowledge of the universe

At this point I shall avoid embarking on what would likely be a long discourse on the nature of science, what it is and what it isn't. Most of this would be unnecessary for our present purpose, which is to explore the consequences of making the bold assertion that *science is an activity of the universe*. But let's first understand what, *in the present context*, I mean by science, which is rather broader in scope than how it is usually represented (also see my discussion of this in Appendix I.)

By science I mean the conscious acquisition and storing (i.e. encoding) of information about the world and, though not always, the conscious application of this knowledge, usually for our advantage in some way. Note that knowledge of the world is not just the pursuit of what we normally think of as 'science'; history, archaeology, geography, and many other areas of knowledge are all embraced by this definition.[87] In fact, *it represents what we all do in our everyday life, from the moment we are born.*

There are a couple of important points to note here. We might say that 'the conscious acquisition and storing of objective information and application of this knowledge' is the same as 'learning'; but 'learning' covers a wider range than this. For example, throughout life we *unconsciously* learn many skills, some basic and others highly complex, as well as appropriate and adaptive ways of responding to a wide variety of circumstances. The same applies to other creatures, but compared to humans, these other creatures at the very most only *consciously* acquire, store, and apply knowledge in a limited way. The second point is that much of the information about the world that our brain consciously acquires and encodes is not derived first-hand. It is communicated to us by other human beings (who may themselves have received that information in the same way). And you and I similarly communicate information we have acquired about the world to others. Again, non-human animals do the same, but in much more limited ways.[88]

The most common way we communicate information is of course through spoken language: every day, we tell people about what has happened in the world (mainly in our daily lives) and *vice versa*. But we also learn a great deal through the

---

[87] Consider also that the acquisition of objective information or 'truth' covers what many professional domains are concerned with—e.g. education, criminal investigation (the police, the legal system etc.), journalism, and anything to do with identifying and rectifying the cause of failure and malfunction.

[88] The conscious acquisition of information by an individual Host may be referred to as a function of 'the biological brain' and the mutual sharing of information a function of 'the social brain'.

written word (now conveyed electronically by such facilities as email and the internet) and through pictures and other forms of imagery (e.g. on television or, again, the internet). Consider, for example, how many famous people you are aware of and what they do or have done. How have you acquired this knowledge? From these people directly? Or how about your knowledge of geography? You are probably aware of quite a few countries, where they are located, their capital cities and, in some cases, details of their history; but how did you acquire such knowledge? How many of those countries have you visited? I would also guess you know a bit about astronomy. You are aware of the planets Uranus and Neptune and maybe some of their moons, the minor planet Pluto, the asteroid belt, planets orbiting other stars, and distant galaxies. At one time, no human being was aware of them but now we are, thanks to telescopes and other devices. And if you are not one of those people who have studied the universe this way, no problem! Ask anyone who has, pick up any book on the subject, watch a television documentary, search the internet, and so on.

Individually and collectively, throughout the millennia that we have been in existence we have consciously accumulated and shared more and more knowledge about the universe (including knowledge of how this knowledge may be processed and interpreted), dramatically so in most recent times. This process is seemingly *relentless*; witness the ever-expanding array of technology that helps drive this forward, the growth of mass communication, mass education, and so on. It is the sharing of knowledge and expertise, consciously acquired by Hosts—a few or hundreds, thousands, even millions—that makes possible these extraordinary developments.

Science as an activity of the universe

Normally we may think of all of this from an anthropocentric standpoint. Here we human beings are, in our minute corner

245

of the universe, observing it, investigating it, understanding and explaining it, and finding out about its past and its likely future. Thus again we think of the universe as something separate from us, something upon which we act and to which we react. Instead, let's adopt a top-down approach, whereby we consider any activity, such as the aforementioned, to be an activity of the universe itself. Viewed this way, isn't it the case that the acquisition of knowledge and its application is part of the fabric and activity of our universe as a whole and just as much a part of the story of its history and evolution as the creation of particles, elements, stars, chemical compounds, planets, life and so on? Does it not, at least in principle, belong to the studies we call astronomy and cosmology? Let's see if we can make a case for saying this.

From our current perspective we can sum up all of this by saying that, over time, at those locations where the universe is consciously aware of its own structure and activity, *it becomes increasingly so*. At least we can make this claim for events on planet Earth; at this locality the universe has become increasingly conscious of other planets in the solar system and the activity taking place on them, likewise other stars, exo-planets, galaxies, and various other structures in far-flung regions of space and time. Here's one illustration: today, potentially every single human being (excluding those unfortunately lacking sight) can look at a map of cosmic background radiation, electromagnetic radiation permeating the universe that originated in the earliest stages of its history. Even if an animal like your pet dog or cat looked at this map, that would constitute 'conscious awareness' of it. This radiation can be listened to and it may be explained in words (which obviously only humans can understand). Once seen, the map may be roughly visualised in its absence. Many scientists spend much of their time studying it. Where else in the universe do these structures (i.e. images) exist? Surely, only at those locations where the universe is actively self-conscious! And there is more to follow.

CHAPTER 34

MORE ON SCIENCE AS AN ACTIVITY OF THE UNIVERSE

Let's continue the discussion by considering not merely the acquisition of knowledge but what people most often think of as 'the achievements of science', namely the practical application of that knowledge. In doing so I shall draw out further the distinction between science as an activity of conscious beings and science as an activity of the universe, viewed from the perspective of universal awareness.

A case example: satellites and other wandering objects
Since its beginnings, the universe has emerged in such a way that at the present epoch in its history there are what we refer to as stars, many with objects we call planets orbiting them; orbiting some of these planets there may be objects which we call moons. We refer to orbiting objects generally as 'satellites'. There are other such objects orbiting stars or wandering around in their vicinity that we call asteroids, meteoroids, and comets. These are composed of materials such as rock, gas and ice, much of which originated in stars that burnt out and exploded.

Now, on our own planet can be found many of these rocky objects that we call meteorites (meteoroids that bombard us from outer space and survive their journey through the Earth's atmosphere). A small minority of these are known to have originally been part of the planet Mars, 40 million miles away. They would have been ejected from the planet by the impact of a large rock or asteroid hitting the Martian surface, and subsequently drawn to Earth by gravity. I think it's safe to say that interplanetary travel by meteoroids is a universal phenomenon and not restricted to our own solar system.

All that I have been describing are what we call 'natural phenomena' that have emerged from the composition and structure of the universe, in accordance with 'the laws of Nature' and with no ultimate intention or purpose save that conceived by the human mind: they just 'happen'.

Now let's consider another type of satellite. These are small scale and largely composed of metal. Like Martian meteors they are ejected from a planet, though not yet, at the time of writing, from Mars. Indeed, according to what we presently know, there is only one such planet, though there could be many more. These satellites often orbit that planet and others. Some of them have landed on other satellites or planets and in a few cases have returned to their planet of origin. Some have travelled longer distances without impacting anywhere.

What am I referring to here? Spacecraft and satellites that originate on planet Earth! From the perspective of the world represented by the human mind we would say that the events described above are the outcome of the accumulation of knowledge and understanding of the world by human beings using the scientific method, and the application of this knowledge both to gain further knowledge and to improve and enrich our lives.

Now consider this. Our reaction to any single instance of what I have been describing is usually to acknowledge and commend the scientists and their technical staff for their achievement. In contrast, if we ever enjoyed the privilege of holding in our hands a meteorite that made its journey to us from the surface of Mars, we would not admire the unknown asteroid for bringing about this feat by crashing into that planet in the required way! But if Nature could tell its own story, then in *neither* of these two cases would it accord such recognition: the distinction that we make, namely *'human-made'* versus *'natural'* would not apply.

Now here's the key point I wish to make: From the perspective of the objective world, whilst it seems almost certain that these metallic satellites and spacecraft are unique to those regions of the universe where conditions are such that it is self-conscious, they are still 'natural phenomena', just like stars, planets, moons, asteroids, and meteoroids. As earlier stated*, they have emerged from the composition and structure of the universe, in accordance with 'the laws of Nature' and with no ultimate intention or purpose save that conceived by the human mind*. So once again we say that any activity, whether it involves 'sentient beings' or not, is activity of the universe itself and may be understood by reference to its properties. [89]

Summary of steps followed

We are going to examine other scientific achievements from the standpoint illustrated by the above example, so let's summarise what we did. Firstly, we took an example of a 'natural' phenomenon in the universe, namely satellites such as moons, and 'wandering objects' such as meteors and comets. Secondly, we looked at 'human-made' equivalents

---

[89] At this point I should confess that I have repeatedly referred to 'conditions in space time where the universe is consciously aware of itself and its own activity' without saying what those conditions are. But much is known about the conditions necessary for the emergence and evolution of life and higher forms of life, and I have no new speculations or revelations to offer in this respect (and no competence to do so).

that arise from knowledge acquired and applied by conscious beings. Finally, we dispensed with the distinction 'natural' versus 'human-made' and considered *all* manifestations of the phenomenon as naturally occurring properties of the universe.

Incidentally, you will have noticed that to convey my arguments I have been relying a great deal on our mind's way of representing the world (in the above case in terms of objects—meteors, spacecraft and so on—and categories such as satellites). As I have stated before, it is much more convenient to express the ideas in this way than otherwise, but from time to time you may find it useful, as I do, to envisage what is being described as part of the seething mass of interconnected activity depicted by our oceanic metaphor of the universe.

'Natural' and 'unnatural' synthesis

Satellites, meteors and spacecraft have collectively provided us with one focus for illustrating what is meant by the assertion 'science is an activity of the universe', but there are many more examples. Let's now apply the above of thinking to another topic and see where it takes us. Consider what science has achieved concerning our understanding of the material composition of the universe and how that knowledge has been applied.

We know that stars like our sun are mainly composed of the elements, hydrogen and helium, which were the first to be created and together still comprise 98% of the visible universe[90] in elemental form. But scientists have discovered that there are over ninety elements to be found in the universe, some extremely rare. How are these elements created? There are also other elements that we say do not occur 'naturally' in the universe. How have *these* been made?

---

[90] The 'visible universe' includes interstellar gas as well as stars; in fact the former predominates.

You may know the answers to these questions, in which case, if you followed the line of reasoning in the last section of this chapter, you will anticipate where this discussion is taking us. Maybe you would like to think about this before reading on.

The answer to the first of the above questions is that these elements are nearly all created in stars. The earliest stars were mainly made of hydrogen, but because of the pressure of gravity the hydrogen is crushed down to make the next heavier element, which is helium. This causes a lot of heat, which is why our sun, or any star, is so hot. And because of all this pressure and heat, heavier elements are created such as lithium, sodium, phosphorus, and metals like aluminium and iron, a process called stellar nucleosynthesis. ('Heaviness' is related to the number of protons and neutrons in the nucleus of an element's atom.) Eventually the star can't hold itself together and it explodes.

To make the heaviest elements requires very special stars and extraordinary events, like two of these special stars ('novae') colliding. This is how gold, for example, is made, and it is why it is comparatively rare. It's the same for silver and platinum and many other rarer elements.[91]

There are however elements that can't be manufactured in this way; their nuclei, being so heavy, would be too unstable and would quickly decay into lighter elements. But that's not the end of the story. On planet Earth, for over eighty years scientists have been synthesising and naming these elements, most of which are too unstable to be of any practical use. Now, it is usually stated that these elements *do not occur naturally*; they are *unnatural*. But, as was argued earlier, this is only how the human mind represents things; in the

---

[91] There is another process, termed 'cosmic ray spallation', whereby lighter elements are manufactured through the impact of cosmic rays on the nuclei of some heavier elements.

real world the distinction 'natural' versus 'unnatural' (or 'artificial', 'synthetic' etc.) has no relevance. Why should it?

To reiterate: hydrogen formed around the time of 'the Big Bang'; heavier elements are synthesised in stars, during cataclysmic events such as a supernova explosion and the merging of nova stars, and by cosmic rays impacting on existing elements. Once again, all these are *activities of the universe that emerge from its composition and structure in accordance with 'the laws of Nature'*. And we may say the same for the creation of the heaviest elements of all; this happens in at least one location in the universe (and probably more) where conditions are such that the universe is conscious of itself and its activity. There is no need to single out the last of these processes as being 'unnatural' or 'human-made'. They too are an activity of the universe and are just another part of the account of how in our universe certain 'particles' (as human mind identifies them) combine to form 'elements' (*ditto*).

In fact we may extend this way of thinking to particles themselves. There are many types of these in the universe (not just protons, neutrons and electrons) some of which are unstable and very short-lived. They are created all over the universe, including on planet Earth, by 'natural' processes whereby existing particles accelerate to near the speed of light, some of which collide with other particles and thus create new particles. Amongst the locations on planet Earth (and maybe other regions where the universe is conscious of itself) in which particle synthesis occurs is in laboratories such as that established by CERN (the European Council for Nuclear Research). As with the creation of the heaviest elements, in our minds we characterise this process as 'artificial' as opposed to 'natural', but from the perspective of the real world there is no such distinction: all is natural.

What about the chemical bonding of elements to form compounds? Traces of compound formation have been detected on cooler stars, including our sun. Many more compounds exist in the space around and between stars, notably those made from hydrogen, oxygen, carbon and nitrogen. On planet Earth there are millions of different compounds that would still be present in the absence of human life (though many are associated with living matter). But human beings themselves are responsible for the synthesis of thousands of other compounds, and these are continually increasing. Adopting our top-down perspective, the creation of *these* compounds, as with any others, is an activity of the universe in those regions where it is conscious of itself and its activity. Thus, once more there is no differentiation *in reality* between natural and unnatural synthesis.

Where the universe is conscious, extraordinary events happen

At this juncture we may feel entitled to say that where the universe is conscious, extraordinary events happen, such as those discussed above and in the previous chapter. Yet I have insisted that we refrain from identifying these events as 'artificial' or 'human-made'. They are all natural activities of the universe that occur elsewhere: they are not *unique*. But the question may have occurred to you as to whether there are events in the universe that can *only* occur at those locations where it is self-conscious. Recall, for example, that in the previous chapter I mentioned the cosmic background radiation and asked where else in the universe do images of this exist except where it is self-conscious.

I have talked about the achievements of scientists in creating particles, elements and compounds that might otherwise not be found on our planet. Perhaps in some cases they are only to be found in the universe where there is consciousness. Other achievements that spring to my mind are: direct and alternating electric currents, laser and fibre optic light, holographic imagery, materials at (almost) absolute zero temperature, and superconductivity. Scientists can tell us if these are known to occur in parts of the universe where no conscious beings exist (e.g. laser light has been detected elsewhere) but it is safe to say that the machines and devices that exploit these emerge only where there is consciousness.

In fact we do not have to consult scientists for answers to our question! Look around and you will see myriads of constructions that are unique to those parts of the universe where there is consciousness—ornaments and furniture in your house, your house itself and your neighbourhood, and more complex structures such as televisions, computers, cars and aeroplanes. And yes, spacecraft and satellites: so far as their activity is concerned, I have equated these with moons, asteroids, meteoroids and comets, but from the standpoint of their physical composition and structure, their occurrence is surely only possible in regions of the universe where there is consciousness. But they are still 'natural'!

CHAPTER 35

THE CONSERVATION AND EXPANSION OF UNIVERSAL AWARENESS

In the previous two chapters I discussed how (at least in our region of the universe) where the universe is self-aware, over time it becomes increasingly so through the evolution of life and individual forms of life, notably sentient beings that I have termed 'Hosts'. I have noted that, from our experience on planet Earth this process of expanding self-consciousness appears to be relentless. It is as though the universe, once it is aware of itself, is driven to become increasingly so. This makes us inclined to ask, 'Well, what's the universe up to in all this? What is its intention or purpose?' But here we fall into the trap of representing reality in anthropocentric terms; intention and purpose are ways we humans interpret our behaviour and that of other sentient creatures, but we will be misled if we think they are applicable beyond that domain. Recall once more that any feature or property of the universe—time, space, matter (stars, galaxies, etc.), energy, and so on (and the universe itself, of course)—may be described as 'emergent', in the sense that it just 'happens' in accordance with Nature. The same may be said of consciousness itself. However, we can strive to understand these phenomena, how their emergence came about, and (since none of them are static) how their emergence has proceeded and will proceed. So, it is entirely valid to ask the question 'What process or processes are driving the universe's inexorable expansion of its self-awareness?'

Before we embark on addressing this question, we may observe the self-reinforcing cycle of increasing awareness: the more self-aware the universe is, the greater its capacity to acquire further self-awareness. Expressing this at the level of Hosts, we have already discussed how our knowledge of world can be applied to create increasingly powerful means of acquiring further knowledge (awareness of the universe). But I think we need to delve deeper into this to arrive at a satisfactory answer to the above question.

Life and evolution

Let's, for a while, remain at the level of individual Hosts and think about how this conscious 'thirst for knowledge' might have emerged. In discussing this, I shall not try to explain consciousness itself; scientists are still a long way from any satisfactory explanation and I have nothing to offer in this regard.

When giving consideration to the above kind of question, scientists often turn to evolution to provide an answer. In the simplest terms, and *as a general rule*, any living thing has a limited life span within which they are usually able to produce offspring with a genetic makeup (genome) resembling their own. Organisms whose genes ensure that they are well-equipped to survive and thrive in their environment will tend to be more successful at reproducing and thus passing on these 'good genes'; thus their offspring will, in turn, also have a better chance of successfully reproducing and passing on these genes. This process is potentiated by 'sexual selection', whereby male and female members of the species compete for mates with 'good genes' (and appear genetically programmed to do so).

It is the property of replication or reproduction that is key for following the present line of thinking. Life did not emerge to fulfil a purpose, but if you ask what an organism's purpose is in existing at all, you are justified in replying 'to produce more copies of its species' (or 'to transmit the recipe for making similar copies of itself'). And to do this it must survive—i.e. avoid death—at least before and during its period of reproductive capacity (or, when there is evidence of altruism, enable other members of the species to do so).

Hence, again in general terms, life itself is relentless in preserving itself and expanding. We see this on our planet: we are astounded by how life forms thrive in the most extreme conditions. Now, you might argue that living material does not present a united front in this respect; there is a life-and-death contest between and amongst most life forms, and virtually all organisms survive by destroying and devouring other organisms. But this is only how an observer construes things. In reality, from a top-down perspective there is no distinction 'predator and prey': 'a lion eating an antelope' or 'an antelope feeding a lion' is an activity of the universe that occurs at a specific location in space-time, where life is thus conserved, not destroyed. Also, consider this: in those rare locations in the universe where there is life, even in the absence of humans extraordinary things exist and take place that, as far as we know, occur nowhere else in the universe. All you need do is gaze around (and look at images of the living world in books and on your television and computer screens) and consider the rich variety of life forms.

Now genes not only influence physical attributes such as size, strength, stamina and general health. They also influence behaviour and behavioural tendencies that are related to survival and reproductive success. These include instinctive responses, temperament (e.g. proneness to aggression or anxiety) and numerous physical and mental abilities and skills. Thus it is understandable how many species come to be genetically endowed with the capacity for curiosity and a predisposition to explore their environment and thus acquire reliable information which may be used for purposes that promote their survival and reproductive success. Those members of such a species who are especially favoured in this regard (and recognised as such by potential mates) are therefore more likely to pass on these genes. And of all species, it is *homo sapiens* that is the most advanced in this respect—i.e. exploring and acquiring information about the environment. This advantage is greatly enhanced by our inherent high level of intelligence, predisposition to socialise, and communicative ability—hence the collective search for information and the sharing of information[92] and its potential applications for mutual benefit.[93]

In bygone days, the above benefits would largely concern the immediate necessities of life such as food, shelter and defence against natural disasters, predators and hostile competitors. Over time, human knowledge and its application have expanded to provide ever more effective means of achieving these goals. That we are warranted in using the term 'exponential' to describe this development, as provided by the comparatively recent dramatic acceleration in improvements in the living standards of most of the Earth's population. Foremost amongst the advances made are those involving the prevention and amelioration of illness

---

[92] Perhaps we shouldn't fail to mention the evidence that plants and trees share information about their environment in a mutually beneficial way, though strictly at the biochemical level.

[93] Some theoreticians have questioned whether consciousness itself plays a role in any of this, the argument being that it is 'epiphenomenal', i.e. it is caused by physical events in the brain but has no effect on physical events itself. This is not the standpoint adopted in this book, which views consciousness as central to the issues under discussion, though in a way that remains to be fully explicated.

and injury, and methods of communication and travel. In all of this, scientific endeavour—the accumulation of knowledge about the world and its beneficial application—has played a key role.

Recall now our original question 'What process or processes are driving the universe's inexorable expansion of its self-awareness?' It seems that one answer may be something like 'the maintenance of life by the evolutionary process'; but further consideration suggests this may fall short of a satisfactory explanation. How do we handle the objection, made by some, that the quest for knowledge, which I have equated with the universe's expansion of self-awareness, is not always related in any obvious way to the promotion of survival and reproductive success, particularly in our modern age? Human beings are more than willing to devote much time, energy and other resources to 'the acquisition of knowledge for knowledge's sake' and experience great fulfilment in doing so. (Perhaps this is comparable to the degree of curiosity displayed by many animal species which goes beyond mere self-preservation.) Many of the accomplishments of science itself, some of which were mentioned earlier, do not seem to have been motivated by the survival needs of those who have contributed to them, likewise those who spend their time learning all about them.

This question is part of a wider debate about what lies behind a large portion of human behaviour that does not seem to have any obvious link with the fundamental aim of protecting and promoting the survival of our species. Other domains of human activity for which consciousness appears to be central include, in all their diverse forms, games (including sport), and art. As participants in these pursuits, we may be active (we play sports and games and we paint and draw; compose and play music, both instrumental and vocal; write stories, poetry and drama; recite or act out these; and so on) or we may be passive observers—watching and listening. Although we can draw some parallels between humans and other animals in these respects, as with the pursuit of knowledge no other creature comes close to us in the physical and mental effort, time and resources we devote to these. Why is this?

The first and most obvious answer is that we enjoy doing them and that is a good enough reason for most of us! But this immediately raises another 'why' question: Why are humans disposed to find them so enjoyable and even compulsive; why, like the acquisition of knowledge, are they so relentlessly pursued and valued? Again we explain their benefit to us in evolutionary terms—sports and games both demonstrate and enhance fitness, and in the arts we have demonstrations of impressive physical and psychological skills.

An alternative explanation is that the performing and observing of these activities have no intrinsic survival value in themselves but make use of innate abilities and behavioural and motivational tendencies that do; it is mere happenstance that we have found ways of utilising these in a manner that bring us such fulfilment. As long as this does not *compromise* the survival of our species in any way, evolution will, in a manner of speaking, adopt a tolerant attitude.[94]

Let's not dwell any further on these matters, which are the subject of much discussion amongst scientists and philosophers.[95] Recall again our original question: 'What process or processes are driving the universe's inexorable expansion of its self-awareness?' My previous answer was *something like 'the maintenance of life by the evolutionary process'* but

---

[94] Evolution or genetic predispositions need not, and I am sure *do* not, lie at the root of *every* behaviour or experience that gives most human beings pleasure. What is the 'survival value' in being thrilled by the view from the top of a mountain, even in a photograph?

[95] See, for example, Greene (2020).

I expressed dissatisfaction with this and in the above discussion I have tried to explain my reasons. Instead, I offer a simpler answer. First we make the observation that, in a manner of speaking, it is the nature of life to endeavour to preserve itself. We then say that the nature of consciousness is *to serve that same purpose* (preservation of life). But now I am saying that *regardless of that purpose*, it is the nature of universal consciousness to strive to preserve *itself* and, in doing so, to expand.

Meditation on the survival of consciousness

Think about the above assertion purely from the standpoint of Hosts like us. Rather than *biological survival* (both as individuals and as a species) being the fundamental driver of our behaviour, what about *survival of our consciousness*? Does this make any sense? Does it work? I invite you to give some thought to this before moving on.

CHAPTER 36

EXAMPLES OF THE CONSERVATION AND EXPANSION OF UNIVERSAL AWARENESS

Human beings are considered to be the only species whose individual members are aware of their own mortality. We know that one day we will die and, of the people whom we know, some will probably die before us. Approaching this rationally, death means that the biological functioning of our bodies ceases and, although some preservation is possible by chemical means, our bodies materially decay, including our brains, and thus we cease to be capable of consciousness.

Now, for the most part we want to remain alive. But consider the hypothetical case of Angela, an otherwise contented person, who knows that soon she will become unconscious and will, unquestionably, remain so for the rest of her life. *Biologically*, however, she will continue to live, perhaps for many years, though only with continuous care. I don't think we would be surprised if Angela declared, 'I might as well die: without any possibility of a return to consciousness, what would be the point of living?'

Of course, too often people feel they have to choose death because the pain and distress of living is too much for them. In other words, being conscious itself is unbearable. But if, given the choice between oblivion and having treatment that enabled them to be consciously alive without experiencing constant pain and distress, would they not choose the latter? In fact, as a generalisation, most people will do what is necessary to maintain their capacity for consciousness (to 'remain a Host') for as long as they are contented. There comes a point when it becomes increasingly questionable whether this urge has anything to do with survival of the species and even whether it does not, in fact, undermine this.

But eventually we all lose our capacity for consciousness by dying. Or do we?[96] Think how, throughout history and across the whole of our planet, humans have invested, and continue to invest, so much time and energy and so many resources, maintaining the belief, against all evidence, that an individual's consciousness survives death and that he or she continues to be aware of what is happening in the world following their departure from it. You will be familiar with the various religious, and indeed non-religious, ideas about an afterlife (including reincarnation) and there is no need for me to describe them here.

The theme of dying will be taken up again shortly. But you will know by now that the idea of an afterlife in the forms envisaged above is not one that is entertained here.

So far, there is probably nothing in this discussion with which you are not familiar. So our next step is to broach these matters from our top-down perspective, namely that (1) the universe is an organic whole; (2) any activity is an activity of the universe; (3) the structure and composition of the universe is such that at certain localities conditions emerge

---

[96] Note that I am for the moment setting aside the theory of universal awareness.

that enable it to be consciously aware of itself and its activity; and (4) it does so increasingly. In anticipation of this, I invite you to pause and think how our exploration of these matters might proceed.

---0---

It is not difficult to translate the information discussed in the previous section into a top-down, universal standpoint. So let's see what further implications and possibilities emerge when we step well back and take this wider perspective. These are quite considerable in number, and far-reaching, but our current knowledge only allows to refer to circumstances on planet Earth.

1. The evolution of consciousness
First, consistent with assertion 1 above, note the acceleration in growth over time of the population of living creatures on our planet that we normally credit with consciousness. Scientists have been able to construct a timeline charting the emergence and evolution of life on Earth since its formation from the debris of exploding or colliding stars around 4.5 billion years ago. This starts with single-cell organisms which appeared around 3.8 billion years ago, followed much later by multicellular organisms of increasing complexity, and then the first animal species, probably around 700 million years ago. We generally think of mammals, by virtue of their brain size and complexity and consequent higher intelligence, as the most likely to be capable of some form of conscious awareness as we understand it. Mammals emerged around 180 million years ago. In terms of biological classification, it seems that other members of the mammalian order to which we belong, namely primates which appeared at least 55 million years ago, *tend* to be more likely than other mammals to exhibit facets and manifestations of *human* consciousness, but not to the extent of humans themselves (*homo sapiens*).

Humans appeared only 300,000 years ago from earlier (and increasingly intelligent) primates. This evolutionary timeline along which we see the emergence of increasingly conscious forms of life, capable of acquiring and applying more and more knowledge of the world, is consistent with our top-down model of the universe's tendency to become increasingly self-aware.

2. The increasing human population

We earlier observed that much of our conscious knowledge of the world, and how it expands, comes through the mutual sharing of this knowledge by Hosts. Our universal perspective predicts that the population of Hosts—human beings, in the case of planet Earth—should tend to grow over time, thereby enhancing the universe's capacity for self-awareness. *Homo sapiens*, as stated, emerged 300,000 years ago and its population has risen since, at a relatively gentle pace until a few centuries ago, since when it has accelerated dramatically, and is now approaching 8 billion. The human population is by far the largest of any primates and may well be the largest of any mammalian species. However, this growth is likely to slow down relatively soon and has already stopped or gone into reverse in some countries. Will this be the end of population growth? Not necessarily, as I shall argue below.

3. The increasing longevity of human conscious life

I have already spoken about the urge, at the level of Hosts, to conserve conscious experience 'for its own sake'. At the universal level, any loss of a Host represents a reduction in the university's capacity to expand its self-awareness, however minute and temporary. (Note how the death of a great scholar, such as an eminent scientist, in the prime of life, is often seen as a serious loss to their field of study.) At present, conservation is only achieved by the Host remaining alive, and the universe's increasing self-awareness has enabled life expectancy to grow substantially, but only up to a limit of around 115 years, to which only a handful of Hosts have come close. The further extension of both average and maximum life expectancy in conscious Hosts is predictable from our perspective of universal awareness. Maybe this will be an indefinite extension if that is possible. Meanwhile, an opportunity that a small minority of Hosts are opting for is cryonics, whereby their head or whole body is frozen at the point of death and kept in that state until such time as doctors may be able to revive it and somehow restore them to normal health. Currently there are doubts about the viability of this practice, but again it is predictable that further knowledge may be forthcoming to make this a workable option.

Another predictable development is the preservation of a Host's consciousness beyond death using computer technology. Scientists are talking about the possibility of, for example, creating a disembodied brain onto which one could upload the mind of an actual person (I am using rather simplistic terms here as this is an area of which I have limited technical knowledge.) The purpose would be the continuation of the conscious experience of being that person (thinking, remembering, imagining, dreaming, etc.) by transfer to a non-biological Host. It is normal at moments like this to say, 'This all sounds like science fiction', but I would bet on its being pushed to the limits of what is scientifically possible.

4. Augmentation of consciousness by computer technology

Computers, as we normally employ them, may correctly be said to have assisted in enhancing conscious awareness and cognitive capacity. Now there is interest in furthering this by 'brain-to-computer (or mind-to-computer) interface', i.e. establishing direct communication between brain activity and an external computer. Alternatively, augmentation of consciousness might be effected by devices attached to the brain itself (in science fiction humans thus equipped are described as 'cyborgs'). These are genuine areas of research by neuroscientists and it is predictable from the standpoint adopted here that they will, over time, be developed as far as is feasible within the laws of Nature.

5. The creation of other kinds of Hosts

Earlier, I gave examples of how universal consciousness enables the replication of certain events and phenomena that occur in other regions of the universe without universal consciousness. Now, universal consciousness is not necessary for the creation of living organisms, non-conscious or otherwise. But scientists appear confident that eventually, enough knowledge will accrue to enable them to replicate, from non-living matter, the simplest carbon-based life forms.[97] From there it may be possible to generate more complex life forms, even conscious beings—i.e. Hosts. If this were done on a grand scale, this would be one way for the population of terrestrial Hosts to increase.

There may be alternatives to carbon-based life—the possibility of silicon-based life is commonly mooted. Perhaps we should be guided by the rule that what is achievable by universal consciousness is limited by what we Hosts term 'the laws of Nature'. However, in theory at least, Hosts need not come in biological form. Universal consciousness has led to the emergence on our planet of what we call 'artificial intelligence', non-biological machines that are equipped with many of the cognitive abilities previously only manifested by humans. This development has greatly facilitated the expansion of our knowledge of the universe (or expansion of universal awareness in the terminology of our model). In the future, will we see the emergence of machines that are

---

[97] Consistent with my earlier discussions I avoid the expression 'artificially-created life'.

conscious of themselves and have a sense of self? This is a much-debated question. How will we know if a machine is thus endowed? Perhaps scientists will be able to devise a physical test for the presence of conscious awareness, but my own feeling is that logically this may not be possible.

I speak with no authority, but my personal opinion is that whatever has emerged in the universe without consciousness may be replicable where there is consciousness.[98] If this is so, then again, it is consistent with the idea of the expansion of universal awareness.

6. Brain-to-brain interfacing

The power and versatility of 'thinking machines' are enhanced if they are linked together and work in tandem. I have previously mentioned the possibility of augmentation of consciousness in human brains by direct linkage with computer technology. How about doing the same with two or more human brains? We can regard this as an extension of what has always happened anyway; as I have said, integral to the expansion of universal awareness is inter-communication amongst Hosts: many minds are better than one. But now we are speaking of interaction at a more direct, physical level—brain hardware if you like ('brain bridging' or 'mindmelding' in the jargon of neuroscientists interested in these possibilities). Again, in terms of our model, this represents a further expansion of the universe's self-awareness, and I again I predict that this process will develop over time, constrained only by what is possible by the laws of Nature.

---

[98] Again, let us not refer to these machines as examples of 'artificial intelligence'. They will emerge, just as we human Hosts have emerged, from the way the universe is structured and functions according to the physical laws of Nature. It is likely that only where there is conscious awareness is this possible. Maybe, new Hosts will eventually emerge through the activities of *these* Hosts (conscious machines making other conscious machines).

7. The migration of Hosts

Bring to mind again that image of the universe as a huge ocean and those regions where its self-awareness has emerged as diffuse patches of light, each with a bright focus indicating the presence of Hosts. Think of that region we know most about: our own planet and solar system. Over time, that area of light is increasing and becoming brighter, indicating that the universe's self-awareness is expanding here. Now imagine that bits of that intense central focus are detaching themselves and moving outwards into surrounding areas, thus 'replicating the focus' elsewhere. What is happening? Hosts are on the move! From our usual perspective, human beings are travelling into outer space.

So far in our history, this has happened only to a limited extent, the most distant journeys being return visits to the Moon. But eventually, people—and maybe also conscious machines—may travel further and establish permanent colonies on other planets in our solar system—new 'central focuses' of brightness as represented by our oceanic metaphor. It is even being suggested that humans may in time be genetically modified to be better able to survive in conditions on other planets. All these developments are in accordance with the relentlessness drive for preservation and expansion that is characteristic of the universe's self-awareness and may be considered as 'natural' rather than 'artificial' or 'human-made'.

8. Inter-planetary exchange of information

It is unknown whether there are regions of universal consciousness other than our own, but it seems very likely, given the huge number of galaxies in the universe, each with a huge number of stars, many of which scientists are now confident have planets. It would represent a major expansion of universal awareness if exchange of consciously acquired information were possible between such regions, but the feasibility of this depends on the distances the information must travel. This exchange may happen somewhere (there may be solar systems in close proximity to one another or with more than one planet in a solar system that is home to Hosts), but the omens are not good for planet Earth. Below, I offer one possible way intercommunication involving terrestrial and extra-terrestrial Hosts may be effected.

9. Overcoming threats to universal awareness

All the future developments that I have outlined are only likely to happen over long periods time—thousands and millions of years. Is there a problem here? Of course! Isn't it likely that intelligent life, including Hosts on planet Earth, will one day, long before any of these advances have had time to get off the ground (in some cases literally!) be obliterated by some global disaster? A huge volcanic explosion? An asteroid impact? A deadly burst of gamma rays from space? A giant solar flare? A world-wide pandemic? We also have what we usually call 'human-made' disasters, the commonly cited ones being global warming and a nuclear war. According to our top-down model these are all activities of the universe and it does not define the last two as 'human-made'; that is, rather than say they occur 'where there are life forms advanced enough to acquire the knowledge to cause these to happen' we say they emerge 'where the universe is sufficiently self-aware'.

So here we have a paradox: whereas expansion of the universe's self-awareness has promoted its survival and further expansion, it is now threatening this through the emergence of global warming and nuclear weapons. But the point is that whatever the threat is, the knowledge consciously acquired enables these threats to be anticipated and either prevented or, if they do occur, their effects to be mitigated. This is a survival advantage for Hosts: no other species is capable of acquiring the knowledge to cure or ameliorate its illnesses or injuries anywhere near the extent

271

that humans do,[99] let alone anticipate the apocalyptic events listed above. Consider, for example, the collision of our planet with a large asteroid or comet. Our accumulated knowledge of the universe informs us that this is an inevitability and may well destroy much of life on Earth including Hosts. Scientists are acquiring more knowledge of how to anticipate such an event and how to forestall it. In terms of our model, we represent this as the universe becoming more self-aware and thus able to further the survival of its self-awareness.[100]

Science has, of course, enabled us to be aware that there are events in the far distant future that will result in the ultimate destruction of consciousness, life itself, and the conditions that make life possible, both locally and, eventually, throughout the entire universe as it continues to expand. The evolution of the Sun will mean that in billions of years from now conditions on Earth will make life unsustainable. By then, Hosts may have already ceased to exist or may have migrated to a more hospitable planet (but only temporarily). Let's consider some more options.

Long before this apocalypse, might terrestrial Hosts abandon Earth and create their own planet orbiting the Sun at a more congenial distance? Could they create another sun that provides the energy they need for survival on their new planet? Could they create several planets and even several solar systems? These suggestions sound ludicrous but remember the principle that where the universe exhibits self-consciousness, structures and processes emerge that occur

---

[99] Self-medication or self-treatment when ill or injured is well documented for a number of species, and chimpanzees are known to treat members of their group (Mascaro *et al*, 2022).

[100] One proposal that might ensure the continuation of life, including Hosts, in the event of an apocalypse, is a 'lunar ark', i.e. the cryogenic preservation of genetic material of all known species of plants, animals and fungi on Earth in underground hollows on the Moon.

elsewhere in the universe without self-consciousness. And by 'a planet' and 'a sun' I do not mean something on the scale of the Earth and our present Sun but constructions that are functionally equivalent to each of these. The International Space Station is a tiny step in the direction of creating another inhabited planet. And at the time of writing, the process of nuclear fusion, which powers the Sun is being replicated on Earth with the aim of using this to generate our energy needs. Alternatively, could humans create roaming rather than orbiting planets?[101] These planets would travel away from our Sun and perhaps eventually leave our solar system altogether (somewhat akin to the Starship Enterprise). Maybe the Hosts inhabiting these 'planets' would not be in the form of human beings but some kind of 'human-made' non-biological intelligence. Perhaps, unlike at present on Earth, the inhabitants of 'roaming planets' would eventually be able to inter-communicate with Hosts on other planets. Who knows?

---

[101] It is believed that there may be billions or even trillions of such 'rogue' planets in our galaxy, though not created by intelligent beings (as far as anyone knows!).

EPILOGUE

All the ideas in this and the previous two chapters could have been presented without any reference to universal awareness at all, and with no loss of validity. Indeed, on any other occasion we would refer to these developments, actual and predicted, as the activities and achievements of many individual conscious beings ('Hosts') such as terrestrial humans, working in collaboration. Instead, we are adopting the standpoint that, just as atoms, stars, planets, elements resulting from nuclear fusion, compounds resulting from chemical reactions, and so on, and life itself, consciousness is a natural process or property of the physical universe that emerges and evolves over time. And what is driving the developments discussed in these chapters is the natural tendency for conservation and expansion of this property, which I have called universe awareness.

What kind of reactions do you have to the futuristic scenarios I have suggested? Speaking for myself, I am tempted to think, 'I probably won't see any of this in my lifetime' and maybe, 'I'm glad (or I'm sad) I won't live to see this.' But then I remind myself that the 'I' that is aware of my thinking these things, the 'I' (Soul [MH]) that is aware of being 'me' (Person [MH]) is universal and not restricted to this one Host. This 'I' *does* experience these events. Hence I might be tempted to think, 'So these events are in store for my future 'me' when Person [MH] has died.' But then I remind myself that MH's timeline of past, present and future is *MH's* creation and ceases when MH dies. There is no universally fixed past, present and future independent of MH or anyone else and therefore no temporal succession of incarnations. All MH or anyone else can say is that these events are consciously experienced by 'I' or, if you don't mind sounding too fanciful, 'Soul [Universe]'. Moreover, there is no way any of us can escape this, and neither is there a beginning or an end to it.

Much of what I have said about the future expansion of universal consciousness is speculative and is constrained by the laws of Nature that govern the universe (it is never satisfactory to say, 'Someday, scientists may find a way of…' when the universe has not). It is nevertheless predictable from our model of universal awareness and its expansion. We presently think of consciousness as an extremely rare occurrence at tiny locations in the vast expanse of our universe. But perhaps over tens of billions of years, universal awareness will escalate and expand to the point where it has a significant impact on the universe's structure and activity, just as it has on planet Earth.

But who knows? For now, we can only gaze at the universe and wonder.

APPENDICES

APPENDIX I

MORE ON REALITY AND THE MIND

In chapter 1 we deliberated on the distinction between 'the real world' and the world created by our brain from information such as light, sound and pressure that impinges on our sensory organs. Here we shall think in greater depth about this distinction. We can do so at three levels.

1. The world through our senses

Firstly, consider how, when we look at the world around us, we see different colours—the sky is blue, grass is green, the Sun is yellow, Mars is slightly red, and so on. But the world in reality is not coloured in this way; it is only the world that our mind creates. Nevertheless, science has revealed that there is still *something* present in the real world, namely electromagnetic radiation of certain wavelengths, corresponding to and correlated with our experience of colour and the varieties of colour we perceive.

Similarly, when we listen to the world we hear all sorts of noises, but the real world isn't noisy in this way. As above, science has shown that *something* exists in the real world

279

associated with sound as we experience it, namely longitudinal vibrations propagated through matter, which for us is most commonly air.

Despite this, we still need to remember that even though we assume that scientific ways of representing these and other phenomena bring us closer to reality, they themselves are still constructions of the human mind and are not reality itself. This is because the images, models, diagrams, and language that scientists use to describe and explain reality still have to be comprehensible to the human mind (including the mind of a scientist!). They may be considered as analogies or metaphors of reality—'as if' ways of thinking and not reality itself. Examples are provided by how scientists conceive and describe natural phenomena such as heat, electricity, gravity (as accounted for both by Newton and by Einstein), the structure of the atom, and 'the Big Bang'.

2. The limitations of our senses

The second level of our deliberations on the present theme is to remind ourselves that we only directly perceive a tiny part of the universe. For instance, no matter how clear the night sky is, virtually all of what we see unaided is a small proportion of stars in our own galaxy (plus the moon and planets, when they are visible and, of course, our immediate terrestrial surroundings). With the aid of instruments such as telescopes and, for tiny things, microscopes we can dramatically increase the information that our sensory organs can detect and our brains can process, thus enhancing our perception and knowledge of the world and what is happening in it. But our senses are still very limited in how they respond. Notably, all around us there is electromagnetic radiation distributed over an enormous range of wavelengths, but we only see that part of the spectrum we call visible light that is emitted and reflected by matter. Similarly, most of the time we see nothing of the molecules of the air that surrounds us, but they are there. Moreover, scientists now tell us that if we take these molecules away, thus creating a vacuum or what we would call 'empty space', at an incomprehensibly microscopic level there is still a seething mass of 'activity'. Also ever-present, but not evident to us, are unattached fundamental particles such as neutrinos; it has been estimated that every second, 100 billion of them pass through each square centimetre of our body, although our senses have no means of detecting them.

At the other extreme, scientists are pretty sure that if we consider the universe in its entirety, most of it would be undetected by us anyway. In order to account for the movement of stars and galaxies, some other kind of substance must exist that we cannot directly observe and which scientists have called 'dark matter'. It has been estimated that this makes up most of the universe. We can be aware of its effects and consequences, but we do not perceive it directly with our senses.

Why, especially, when unaided, are our sensory organs, our brain, and the rest of our nervous system so limited? One answer is that they only do what is necessary and no more; they have evolved to serve the fundamental requirements of enabling and furthering our individual survival and that of our species—the passing on of our genes. The same principle applies for any organism.

Now suppose, as is likely, that there are intelligent beings in other parts of the universe and that they manage to survive and procreate in environments very different to our own. *Their* nervous systems will have evolved for them to flourish in *those* environments, say by being receptive to different portions of the electromagnetic spectrum than we are. Their brains will be adapted to process this information and hence they will perceive, experience and understand the world in ways different to us. Maybe some will have sensory systems that are more advanced than ours, and brains that have significantly greater processing capacity. Now consider what could arise if, living in their communities, there were a minority of such beings, the structure and functioning of whose nervous systems more closely resembled those of us terrestrial humans. Would these individuals not be considered by the majority to be inferior in some way, with their limited and distorted ways of perceiving and understanding the world? Perhaps they would be identified and labelled as having some kind of disorder, just as we on Earth have names for people whose perception and understanding of the world is also limited and distorted compared to that of the majority—for example people with serious mental illnesses and intellectual impairments?[102]

This is a sobering thought and one that scientists and philosophers are well aware of. But there are two considerations that are sometimes overlooked, both of which highlight the fact that in the process of acquiring knowledge and understanding of our world, our brains do not work in isolation. Firstly, we record and share—i.e. *communicate*—our observations and expertise with one another and secondly, particularly in recent years, we have developed 'artificial intelligence'—machines that are increasingly adept at thinking for us, including performing mathematical operations and calculations. Both of these, along with our increasingly powerful instrumentation for observing our world, characterise the enterprise we call 'science'. Yet, as stated earlier, all that we observe, understand and

---

[102] On Earth, blindness and deafness amongst humans are obviously disabilities but people so affected may still lead full and rewarding lives. It's worth thinking about what makes this possible and what its implications are for the present discussion. Worth considering also is the question, 'If there are intelligent beings on another planet who have no need for vision or hearing, what would be the implications for *their* worldview?

communicate must still be represented in a form that our sensory systems can convey to our brain, our brain can construct and process, and our language can express.

3. So what does the world *really* look like?

There is a third stage in our deliberations on 'the two worlds'—objective and subjective—and this takes us deeper into the mystery of the true nature of reality. Consider this question: 'If the world that I perceive is not the real world, but only the one I construct in my mind, then what does the real world *actually* look like?'

The answer to this question is that the world itself does not *look like* anything. The property 'looking like' is something conferred on the world by the person, or any creature for that matter, who is doing 'the looking'. So it is meaningless to ask what the world looks like in the absence of anyone looking at it![103] Also bear in mind this: when you see a visual representation of the universe—the stars and galaxies, etc.—or when you create one in your mind, it will always be a view from a fixed point, namely where the observer is or is presumed to be, with the stars and galaxies being at varying distances from that point of view.[104] But if we are trying to think about the universe as it is and not as it is observed, there will be no 'point of view'; the view of the universe will, as it were, be 'from nowhere' (or maybe you could say 'from everywhere at once'). Can you construct this

---

[103] Thus we encounter, not for the only time in this book, a question which is meaningful when asked of the world we construct in our minds, but not of the real world.

[104] Also, the observer will be located at a specific *time* as well as a specific place ('a specific point in space-time'). We must also bear in mind that he or she will not be observing how the universe is at that specific time; the further away the stars and galaxies, the further back in time they are relative to the observer, since the light they emit can only travel at a finite speed.

283

in your mind? I can't! In fact, the same can be said when we look at any object, however large or small. Blackburn (1999) presents a nice puzzle relating to this. You are asked to imagine a room in which there is a vase of flowers on a table some way in front of a mirror attached to one of the walls. You are not to imagine being in this room yourself. Is the vase of flowers in the mirror? I'll give the answer later.

Overview

It may now help to spell out the position adopted in this book concerning the 'two worlds' distinction.

1. There is a real world that exists whether you or I or anyone else is experiencing it. Let's call anything in the real world 'O' (for 'objective').

2. The world that we observe and experience is constructed from information from O (light waves, sound waves, chemical emissions, etc.) impinging on our sensory organs and conveyed to our brain where it is processed, thus in some way giving us a conscious representation of what is 'out there'. Let's call this conscious representation 'S' (for 'subjective').

3. We can go further than this. Suppose, for example, that O is something in the real world and, when you look at it, you experience it as an ornament (S). So it is not that S is nothing more than a construction of the brain itself, as in the case of imagination or dreaming. Now, whereas S tells us that O is 'a thing', S itself is not 'a thing': it is an *activity* you are performing[105] (this is discussed in detail in chapter 6). In fact,

---

[105] For convenience, for much of this discussion I talk about S as though it were indeed 'a thing', but it is important to keep in mind that it is 'an activity', something we do. Also worth reminding ourselves is that although I talk about 'the subjective (S) versus the objective (O) world' as though they are separate, S must be part (strictly an activity) of O, the real world * the real world).

we can say that S is an activity involving O (whatever the 'ornament' is in the real world), your sensory organs, and your brain. (This activity includes the reflecting of light waves by O that are received by your two retinae, resulting in impulses being conveyed along your optic nerve fibres. Hence we could expand the range of components that are involved in the activity of experiencing S, such as the source of the light—the Sun or an electric lamp. These are considerations for exploration later in our journey.)

Thus you 'see' O. You might also touch O and smell it, and even taste it with your tongue. In these terms, S is still an activity, not 'a thing'. When you turn your attention away from O, you cease to 'do S', except that you might continue to hold an image of S in your mind. When you again attend to O you resume 'doing S'. Another person with you who is attending to O will be 'doing' his or her own S. In the absence of any observer—i.e. when no sentient being is 'doing S'— O still exists in reality, but there is no S.

4. When you attend to O, you experience it as having various attributes, principally that it is 'an object' that occupies a fixed position in space and has a certain size, shape, brightness, colour, feel and maybe smell. However, you can only say that these are the attributes of *your S*; you are not entitled to say that they are attributes of O. Just as S is not a *reproduction* of O itself, neither are the individual attributes or 'qualities' that you perceive.[106] But O is *something*

---

[106] Some philosophers distinguish between primary and secondary 'qualities' of an object. Primary qualities, such as size, shape and motion, are intrinsic to the object and don't require an observer. Secondary qualities, such as colour, taste and smell, are responses of the observer to the object. According to the present way of thinking, each of these primary qualities exists in some form in the absence of an observer, but how they are represented in the mind does not match how they are in reality. Thus the primary-secondary distinction tends to disappear.

'out there' in the real world and so are the properties that give rise to those fundamental attributes of S listed above. For example, as stated earlier, the colours of S are related to the frequencies of light emitted or reflected by O. In other words, S contains information about O (though the processing of this information by the observer will vary in reliability—consider, say, the phenomenon of optical illusions).

5. Thus we might say that 'S is O in coded form.' Chapter 1 provides a more specific analogy that may assist here, so long as we bear in mind that all analogies are limited and are apt to mislead us if we treat them as literal equivalents. We can think of S, our subjective representation of our world, as like a map of a country. The country itself is O, external reality. Now a map can be accurate, highly detailed, and up to date but there is no way we would claim that it is a reproduction of the country it represents or its various elements and attributes; hence the expression 'The map is not the territory'. (Strictly speaking, we should say that an everyday map is a representation not of O itself but of S, a representation of O.) Hills, valleys and plains may be represented (encoded) by different shades of green and brown; lakes and rivers are usually blue shapes and lines; roads and tracks may be marked as black lines of varying thickness; places of significance may be identified by various icons and words; and so on. Except in the most trivial sense, none of these bears any resemblance to anything about the country itself. Nevertheless the features and attributes that they represent, in a consistent manner, actually exist in that country; they are not, as it were, illusory. Hence, 'if it's on the map, it's part of the territory' is a useful rule of thumb.[107] In

---

[107] Exceptions to this are experiences such as dreams and hallucinations (but not illusions) for which there is no sensory input.

other words, a map should provide us with reliable *information* about the country.

A good map is one that best enables us to successfully navigate the territory in which we find ourselves; hence there are different maps that are suitable for different purposes, some being, say, more detailed than others. As a rule however, the more information there is on a map, the more you can learn about the territory it represents just by studying the map itself. But the map can only be constructed by making detailed observations of the territory itself.

In all these ways S is akin to map of O, but the analogy is limited by the fact that it is relatively easy to compare a map for accuracy with the territory it represents; the relationship between S and O is clearly more complex (see point 6 below). Also, while an ordinary map does not consider that the map-reader is part of the territory it represents, any sentient creature observing the universe is itself part of the universe.

6. The forgoing is consistent with an assertion I repeatedly make in this book, namely that by exploring our world in a systematic and rational manner, as science does, we learn more about the nature of reality itself. In our present terminology, it is the means whereby we can improve our map so that it is more consistent with the territory that it represents.

7. Especially in recent times a remarkable consequence of scientific exploration is the acknowledgement that what S is telling us about O may be quite erroneous in the most fundamental of ways. This applies to our notions of time and space. For example, scientists now know that, in contradiction to our everyday understanding (our everyday map of reality), the rate at which time is 'flowing' is not consistent across all points in space and depends on local conditions such as the strength of gravity. Similar considerations apply to our concept of space. Hence S gives us a misleading representation of O and, in order to progress

in our understanding of the real world, we need to set aside some fundamental ideas that we normally take for granted. I have more to say about this towards the end of this appendix.

The context of this discussion

The matters that we have been discussing have been debated by philosophers for centuries and in more recent times have received increasing attention from neuroscientists, physicists and other learned people who are interested in the nature of consciousness. As is to be expected in science, there are different ideas and theories, in some cases contradictory. The opinions of some of these scientists, who I must stress are considerably more informed than I am, are consistent with the position I have adopted here, whereas those of other scientists are incompatible. For example, some would go as far as to assert that in reality there are no such things as time and space (or space-time). The position this book takes is that time and space exist in reality in some form ('if it's on the map, it's part of the territory') but our subjective experience of them is only a coded representation.

Despite this, I am confident that all scientists would agree that the way we perceive the world is determined by how our sensory organs and nervous system are constructed and function and is such as to enable us to deal effectively with our environment, principally in evolutionary terms—i.e. from the standpoint of survival both of our individual selves and our species. Some scientists (e.g. Hoffman, 2019) express this more strongly by asserting that this means that evolution *prevents* us from perceiving reality objectively since that would compromise survival. Others argue that we do perceive the world realistically, as this is *advantageous* to our evolution.

My position is more consistent with the former stance. However, I believe that some scientists overplay the role of evolution here and seem at times to be saying that there is a choice between perceiving the world as it is in reality and perceiving it as is conducive to successful evolution. In my opinion it is not possible for any physical object, natural or otherwise, that is capable of consciousness to create for itself an exact reproduction—a view from nowhere—of the objective world, evolution or no evolution. And I mean this from a logical standpoint. In fact, if you push me, I would go even further and say it is *meaningless* to think of the universe in this way. The best *I* can say (you might do better) is that through our scientific exploration of our universe we can gradually gain a more accurate representation of how it *behaves*. But all that can be said about its actual appearance, including anything in it, is that it 'just is'.

I should also add here that some philosophers (and even some scientists) would also dispute the claim that studying the physical world as we subjectively experience it (which is all we can do), even in the disciplined manner typified by science, brings us nearer to understanding the reality. For example, one neuroscientist (Hoffman [2019] again) considers that our subjective representation of the world is akin to an icon on the dashboard of a computer that links to a file. Studying the properties of the icon (e.g. size, shape, colouring and patterning) tells us nothing about the file to which it is linked. According to the position I have outlined, this is a false analogy. It is true that the computer icon contains no information about the file, but S, our subjective experience, does contain information about what it represents in the real world, and studying it will certainly tell us more about the latter (consistent with our map-territory analogy).

Scientific versus everyday ways of thinking

It is commonly asserted that the way scientists reason and think about the world is different from that of people in general (what we might call 'common sense'). I have already mentioned that the insights and discoveries of scientists, particularly in recent years, are sometimes at odds with our everyday ways of understanding the world, even at times appearing to contradict basic logical assumptions that we take for granted. One reason for this is the development of technology that enables us to detect and record far more information about the world than we are otherwise capable of doing. Thus scientists have demonstrated unequivocally that at the extremes of such physical properties as size, time, distance, mass, velocity and acceleration, the world behaves in ways that are unpredictable from, and even contradictory, not just to previous scientific understanding but also our everyday knowledge and ways of thinking.

Now, it is certainly true that 'the scientific method' demands a very disciplined way of thinking and reasoning, but I would argue that this is not so different from what human beings in general are capable of doing when coping with everyday life, notably ensuring their personal survival and ability to procreate. From the cradle onwards (especially in our formative years) we discover and accumulate more and more information about the world around us (we 'enrich our map of the territory') and consequently we must amend our understanding of it. So what made sense to us in the past may no longer do so today, and *vice versa*.

Hence, it may be better for the purposes of our present deliberations to think more generally in terms of 'acquisition of knowledge by humans', rather than narrowly in terms of science and scientists. This theme is developed further in the final chapters of this book.

As an aside, it may be worth contemplating that until recently, our lack of awareness of what modern science has revealed to be fundamental limitations in the way we understand the world did not threaten our survival and reproductive potential. But this is no longer the case, now that we rely on applications of these discoveries in our daily life. For example, there would be dire consequences for us if our satellite navigation systems did not allow for the tiny effects of the Earth's gravity on the passage of time.

Back to the mirror and vase puzzle

So now is the time to return to the puzzle described earlier about imagining a room containing flowers and a mirror but without you in it. If your answer to the question is that the flowers are in the mirror then you can only create the image with you being located at certain viewing points, likewise if you say the flowers are not in the mirror. Hence neither can be the view from nowhere, as required by the exercise. And if you say that the flowers come and go in the mirror, your viewing point must be moving around the room! Could any intelligent being or machine successfully perform this task? I don't think so.

APPENDIX II

MORE MEDITATIONS ON PERSONAL IDENTITY

Two more thought experiments are presented here on the themes introduced in Part III. I constructed both of them myself but I would not be surprised if other people have as well. I hope they bring out clearly for you the implications of what we have discussed for the question of preservation of personal identity. In the case of the first of these I must apologise to you for the distressing nature of the scenario which I am asking you to consider.

Suicide by teleportation

Consider the dilemma of someone whom we shall call Hal. Sadly, Hal has reached a point in his life when he doesn't want to carry on anymore: he says, 'I want *out*.' Being a rationalist and having no religious beliefs he is satisfied that death means an end to his awareness of being—in other words oblivion or 'unconsciousness for ever'. This is exactly what he is yearning for. But he has a dilemma: he is acutely aware that his suicide will cause unbearable grief and unhappiness to his loved ones, including his dependants, and friends. Is there any way of avoiding this?

As it happens, Hal is living at a time in our future when teleportation is a reality and he has followed the reasoning behind the thought experiments discussed in Part III, namely that a person to be teleported is effectively killed—his or her awareness of being ends, though the person he is continues as normal (recall the faulty teleportation scenario with you waiting on the Moon to be annihilated while the teleported you is safe on Earth, unaware that anything is amiss). To Hal, teleportation would seem to be a very satisfactory way out. Person [Hal] will still be around to carry out his responsibilities to his family, friends and colleagues; nobody will be shocked by his death and mourn his passing. 'But,' he reasons, 'I'll no longer be aware of being Hal—it's as though "someone else" will be. For "me now", it will be oblivion.' For this purpose Hal needn't be transported to the Moon of course; we can imagine that the teleportation is from one chamber to another in the same building.)

If—and I hope this never happens—you were in the same state of mind as Hal and had the same intention, would you feel this offers you a satisfactory way out of your problems, preferable to ending your life in a conventional manner? I invite you to think about this before proceeding.

My response (and if you disagree with me that's entirely in order) is that it seems pointless. The whole purpose of Hal's undergoing the teleportation exercise is to put an end to Soul [Hal], his awareness of being this unfortunate person. But once the teleportation scenario is completed, to the teleported Hal it would seem that nothing has happened, even though it appears from our deliberations that Soul [Me before teleportation] would indeed have ceased to be. I think that if Hal were cognisant of all of this he would decline this method of suicide.

Let us just for the sake of argument take this further and make the reasonable supposition that prior to teleportation, the person needs to be rendered unconscious by a general anaesthetic. Since Hal is exactly replicated, he will still be under the anaesthetic when he is reconstituted in the reconstruction chamber and will need time to regain consciousness. Now imagine that the operators merely carried Hal, while unconscious, from the deconstruction chamber to the reconstruction chamber. How would he, on regaining consciousness, or anyone else, be able to tell the difference between the outcome in this scenario and that when teleportation had actually taken place? There would be no way whatsoever. Yet our earlier thought experiments indicated that, if the teleportation had taken place, the original Hal would have died.

I shall leave you to think about the variation of the teleportation scenario where, owing to a glitch, Hal is aware that his destruction has yet to take place, but the reconstituted Hal is now conscious and aggrieved that nothing appears to have changed.

The replicated brain dilemma

Now please consider this thought experiment. Imagine that right now you are participating in a laboratory experiment in which scientists have wired your brain to a machine that is precisely equivalent to your brain (maybe another biological brain or maybe a computer) and this machine is detecting *and replicating* exactly all the activity of your brain. Let's say that the scientists have given this machine the nickname 'Miranda' (meaning 'to be wondered at').

Since we have taken the view that all conscious experience is an outcome of the activity of the brain, we can reasonably assume that Miranda, by replicating exactly the activity of your brain, is experiencing consciousness, and that all of its conscious experiences (what it sees, hears, feels, thinks, remembers, etc.) must be *exactly* the same as yours, no more and no less than this.

Let us be clear that all you would be experiencing in this experiment is, say, lying on your back with your head in a scanning device, maybe continuously hearing one or more loud noises, but otherwise letting your thoughts drift idly by. Probably you would be looking forward to when the scientists announce that the experiment is over, and you can collect your well-earned participant's reward and get on with the rest of your day, feeling none the worse for the experience.

But suppose that during the experiment you ask yourself these questions: 'Am I ...... *(your name)* or am I Miranda?'; 'Would I allow the scientists to turn Miranda off when they announce that they've finished?'; and 'What would I experience if they did turn Miranda off?' I invite you to think about these questions now and decide on your answers before going any further.

I have presented this thought experiments to quite a number of people, some of them very knowledgeable about the brain, and everybody has their own way of answering the questions posed. I have my own answers and surprisingly few people come up with them, but (I hope you don't think I'm boasting here) after some discussion with me more of them come round to my way of thinking. Others are absolutely convinced that I am wrong and they are right. I find this very interesting. What I have learnt from this is that to a surprising degree we differ in the ways we think about and understand profound issues such as the meaning of 'self', 'personal identity', and 'awareness of being'. This accounts for why we have our own way of answering the questions and how difficult it may be for us to understand why other people come up with answers that are different from our own. And it does not mean that only one of us must be right and everyone else wrong. So here are my answers.

When I (MH) ask myself the question *Am I MH or the Miranda?* my answer is that I don't know, since both will be having exactly the same conscious experiences (recall that we are adopting the premise that *all conscious experience is an outcome of the activity of the brain*). Nobody can help me with this, not even the scientists present. Consequently I might not want them to turn off Miranda in case I *am* Miranda and therefore they are exterminating me. But when they do turn off Miranda, as they must, inevitably I (as MH) breathe a sigh of relief because it will now seem to me that when I was asking myself the question 'Am I MH or Miranda?' I was indeed MH. But if I *was* Miranda when I asked this question, the outcome would have been *exactly* the same! No other outcome is possible.

Once again I have no means of determining whether I am the original me or a replicated me, even when, on this occasion, the replicated me is exterminated. And again this appears to contradict our assumption that our 'Soul', our awareness of self, is constant and defines our personal identity and its preservation over time.

APPENDIX III

THE BODY, THE MIND AND THE UNIVERSE

Suppose there is a woman, Sheena, and that somewhere else in time and space there is another person called Sheena. Let's call these two people Sheena 1 and Sheena 2. Suppose that Sheena 2 is physically identical, atom for atom, to Sheena 1. For present purposes it does not matter whether this is possible in reality. What are some consequences of this?

Clearly, the two Sheenas must be completely indistinguishable in their appearance and be having identical experiences as we are imagining them. So what they are doing, what they are perceiving, thinking and remembering, and so on, and how they are feeling, must all be *precisely* the same.[108] Any differences would mean that they are not identical, atom for atom. So let's say Sheena 1 is sitting in her garden. Sheena 2 must be doing likewise, and the two gardens must be absolutely identical. If, for example, in Sheena 2's garden there is a rose bush whereas in Sheena 1's garden, in the same location there is a hydrangea, then the brain activity of the two Sheenas associated with their perception of their

---

[108] Perhaps the two Sheenas would have to be in separate universes.

299

gardens would be different, likewise their memories associated with the respective plants.

They must indeed have identical memories and therefore identical life histories. Hence Sheena 2's mother and father must be identical to Sheena 1's; therefore their grandparents must be identical; and so on and on back in time. Obviously their husbands must be identical, and hence their husband's parents, and so on.

Now let's suppose that during the course of her life, Sheena 1 has travelled widely and is well acquainted with the physical and political geography of the planet on which she lives. Since Sheena 2 must have had identical experiences and must possess the same knowledge as Sheena 1 (otherwise, for one thing, their brains would be, different, however slightly), there is a compelling argument that in order for the two Sheena's to be identical, the two planets on which they live must also be identical.

Let's now suppose that Sheena 1 is gazing up at the night sky, cloudless and with minimum light pollution, with a moon and the stars of the galaxy they belong to clearly visible. Sheena 2 must be enjoying this experience too, and what her visual system is relaying to her brain must be identical to that experienced by Sheena 1. In fact, let's suppose that Sheena 1 is an astronomer and has a powerful telescope at her disposal, which allows her to see galaxies beyond her own; likewise, therefore, Sheena 2. Both Sheenas will also have exactly the same extensive knowledge, including that gained from other scientists' descriptions and images, of the structure of their universe, its history and its origins. Hence those parts of the universe of which each are both aware must be identical. Does this not also require that the other, far greater parts of the universe of which they have no direct or indirect awareness also have to be identical? If they were different, would this not mean that there would be differences in the parts of their universes of which they *are* both aware? Perhaps so.

Now consider one more idea. Suppose that Sheena 1 has with her a book on cosmology that is open at a page on which there is a map that scientists on her planet have created of their universe's cosmic background radiation, electro-magnetic radiation that permeates their universe and which has its origins in the earliest stages of its history. As with all other of Sheena 1's perceptions, Sheena 2 must also have sight of this map, *which must be exactly the same as Sheena 1's.*

It is difficult to escape the conclusion that, just from the stipulation that Sheena 1 and Sheena 2 are to be absolutely identical, down to the last atom, Sheena 1's universe must be wholly, or in large part, identical to Sheena 2's universe. If there *were* differences they would be reflected in differences in the physical composition of the two women, however microscopic in scale.

If that is correct, is there not another extraordinary conclusion that we may consider, namely that, either directly or indirectly, in the physical constitution of both Sheenas, most notably their brains and nervous systems, is the detailed structure of the universe, either in part or in its entirety, which they each inhabit? And if this is so, mustn't it apply also to anyone else in the universe, including you and me? Let me expand on this point.

By the expression 'represented in some way' I mean the exact arrangement of the trillions and trillions of atoms that comprise your brain at any moment. The question is 'If something in your universe, howsoever tiny, were to be different, wouldn't this always be represented by a difference, howsoever tiny, in the arrangement of those atoms that comprise your brain?' For everyday experiences we would say the answer is yes. Say that at the moment you are aware of a fly buzzing around you. Now, if the fly were not present—a miniscule difference in the universe you inhabit—then the atoms of your brain would at that moment be ever-so-slightly differently arranged. But it's not just a difference in your universe 'at that moment'; may we not also say 'your universe up to and including that moment' (since any difference in the universe 'at that moment' must arise from things being different before 'that moment', and so on back in time?

How far can we take this reasoning? Think of gazing up at the stars on a clear night and going through the same process. Or looking at the map of the cosmic background radiation. Is the answer to the above question always 'Yes'?

APPENDIX IV

THE UNIVERSE AS ONE: SOME DIGRESSIONARY CONSEQUENCES

As we have proceeded along our journey, we have had increasingly to take account of the fact that we, the observers of the world, are parts of the world itself, and I imagine that we would all agree that nothing that we do occurs in isolation to the rest of the universe. But neither would we ordinarily go to the other extreme and say that everything we do is activity of the universe itself. Yet this is the conclusion I offered you in chapter 26 and I invited you spend some time thinking about your life from this perspective. Now let's explore this idea with some more examples.

Anthropomorphism

As I have noted elsewhere in this book, as human beings we cannot fail to contemplate our universe—our own planet and moon, our solar system, all the stars in our galaxy and so on—and find it all so astonishing, fascinating, and mysterious. Also recall that in chapter 5 I talked about the human brain and what an astonishing object it is, possibly the most amazing thing in the universe. I added however that 'We should be cautious about describing anything in the universe as "remarkable," "extraordinary," or "special," as these qualities only exist in our subjective ways of categorising and judging things.' In other words, we should avoid being 'anthropocentric'.

Related to this, I have at times talked about what an amazing coincidence it seems that any event that we choose to think about occurs at all ('the unlikeliness of anything'), since a myriad of other events or circumstances would have to occur or be in place to ensure that that one event also happens. This applies to our own existence as an individual, the existence of life on planet Earth, and the fact that life is possible at all anywhere in our universe. Again at such times I have reminded you that the quality of 'amazingness' resides not in the external world itself, but within the person making the observation.[109]

As an aside, this happens in everyday life. For example, when you tell me that you find a person 'interesting' it means that **you** *are interested* in them. If you describe someone as 'annoying' it means **you** *are annoyed*. If you say a film is 'boring' it means **you** *are bored*. If you say something is 'moving' (in the emotional sense) **you** *are moved*; likewise, 'astonishing', *astonished*; 'fascinating', *fascinated*; 'mysterious', *mystified*; and so on.

Implicit in this process is a separation between we humans ('Hosts') and the universe that we inhabit; we are, as it were, observers of the universe, perceiving it, reacting to it, explaining it, and dealing with it in some way. And all the above—being amazed, being moved, being astonished and so on—are *activities* that *we* engage in. However, we are now

---

[109] Given the abundance of planets in the universe, it is not so extraordinary that there is at least one on which conditions are ripe for human beings to thrive and who may be tempted to be amazed that so many things are just right for them to exist at all. The same argument applies if, as some scientists believe, ours is one of many universes, not all of which have the right combination of properties to enable the emergence of intelligent life.

thinking of ourselves as parts of the universe and everything we do as activities of the universe: there is no separation. So when we say that the universe is aware of itself and its activity, we include in this activity its being amazed, moved, astonished, fascinated, etc., by itself and what it does. (And these activities include its being astonished, fascinated and mystified by its ability to be conscious of all of this!) Moreover, we might even say that, very occasionally, the universe admonishes itself for being anthropocentric, e.g. forgetting that 'astonishment' denotes the activity of being astonished and is not some inherent quality of the universe itself! (Or maybe this is too paradoxical a claim. More often, we speak in a similar manner about our brain being fascinated and mystified by how it works.)

Now recall that in Part V we noted that human beings have an automatic predisposition to perceive the universe as millions of separate objects and to classify them and give them names and identities, likewise with activities. According to the philosophy underpinning this book, this is how the human brain constructs reality from the information arriving through its senses, but we are not entitled to claim that this separation and classification of objects and activities exists in the universe outside of the human mind (or maybe we should say the mind of any sentient being). While we can still adhere to these principles, we are now insisting that 'the human mind' is itself an activity of the universe. We can therefore acknowledge that the classification of objects and activities is something the universe does at the level of Hosts. And *in that particular sense only* it is 'objective reality'. Incidentally, as I describe in the final chapters of the book,, we may apply the same thinking to the distinction 'natural' versus 'unnatural' (or 'artificial', 'synthetic', 'man-made', etc).

This way of thinking extends to our perception of time. To reiterate: our position is that the universe does not have a past, present, or future whereby only what is in the present exists objectively. Past, present, and future are the private experiences of each Host, the 'before', 'now', and 'after' that relate to the Host's ongoing conscious experience or discrete conscious event. However, we must now acknowledge that experiencing past, present and future existence is an activity of the universe *at the level of Hosts*.

In summary, *according to our earlier thinking*, our perceptions of our world, our evaluations of it, our emotional reactions to it, our interpretations of it, and our ways of understanding it do not belong to the universe but rather are what we mentally *impose* on it. *Now* we are thinking of them as activities of the universe itself. So long as we keep to that particular way of thinking ('at the level of Hosts'), then we can indeed say that they are 'properties of the universe'. And amongst these properties is the ability of the universe to ask itself those fundamental questions 'How?' and 'Why?'

REFERENCES

Blackburn, S. (1999) *Think: A Compelling Introduction to Philosophy*. Oxford: Oxford University Press.
This book, authored by a well-respected philosopher, is a very good introduction to several of the themes pursued in the present book, such the mind, knowledge and reality, and the meaning of self or personal identity.

Damasio, A. (2000) *The Feeling of what Happens: Body, Emotion and the Making of Consciousness*. New York: Vintage Books.

Dawkins, R. (1998) *Unweaving the Rainbow*. Boston, MA: Houghton Mifflin.

Greene, B. (2020) *Until the End of Time: Mind, Matter, and our Search for Meaning in an Evolving Universe*. London: Allen Lane.

Hoffman, D.D. (2019) *The Case against Reality: How Evolution Hid the Truth from our Eyes*.

Lovelock, J. (2000) *Gaia: A New Look at Life on Earth*. Oxford: Oxford University Press.

Mascaro, A., Lara M., Southern, L.M., Deschner, T. & Pika, S. (2022) Application of insects to wounds of self and others by chimpanzees in the wild. *Current Biology*, **32**, R112-R113.

McTaggart, J.E. The unreality of time. *Mind*, **17** (No. 68) 457-474.

Oakley, D.A. & Halligan, P.W. (2017) Chasing the rainbow: The non-conscious nature of being. *Frontiers of Psychology*, **8**, 1924.

Parfit, D. (1984) *Reasons and Persons*. Oxford: Oxford University Press.

Rosenthal, D. (2005) *Consciousness and Mind*. Oxford: Oxford University Press.

Printed in Great Britain
by Amazon

84813675R00180